Amazon Echo Dot

The Ultimate User Guide to Amazon Echo Dot for Beginners and Advanced Users (Amazon Echo Dot, user manual, step-by-step guide, Amazon Alexa, smart device)

Amazon Echo Dot
The Ultimate User Guide to Amazon Echo Dot 2nd Generation for Beginners (Amazon Echo Dot, user manual, step-by-step guide, Amazon Echo user guide)

ANDREW HOWARD

AMAZON ECHO DOT

The Ultimate User Guide to
Amazon Echo Dot
2nd Generation for Beginners

Andrew Howard

CONTENTS

Introduction

The Second Generation Amazon Echo Dot has got a sleeker design with updated features. It has more powerful speech processor and also comes with Echo Spatial Perception (ESP). It's very helpful when there are multiple Alexa devices in the same home. But the closest device responds first. If you need more than one Amazon Dot you can order 6 and get 1 free. You can also buy 10 and get 2 free for a bigger house or for the gifts to your friends and relatives.

Amazon Echo Dot has got a lot of new updates and functions. This smart device is a game changer as it has a compact design and small price. Now Amazon Dot can do much more, for example, it can call an Uber, control your home or even order Domino's pizza. Besides, the updates to Dot are sent automatically. Second Generation Amazon Echo Dot is able to adapt to speech patterns, personal preferences and vocabulary.

This device is presented in two colors: black and white. As for more sophisticated customers, you can also choose it in various leather and fabrics to blend in with any environment. You can just use it for any room. But if you desire only to get Dot as a part of a bundle, these bundle functions may be used along with the Bose Soundlink Mini II, the Phillips Hue Starter Kit, the TP-Link Smartplug, or the ecobee3 Smart Thermostat. These appliances are able to control many things in your home only with the help of your voice. For example, changing thermostat settings or altering home lighting.

No matter in which room you are, this device is able to accept your orders. Even if music is playing it has ability to recognize your voice. This advantage is possible due to the seven built-in far-field microphones that is used for hands-free-control. You can awake Dot by saying simply the word "Alexa". The device is ready to perform your order if you see the blue ring on its top. It indicates the device is turned on. The Echo Dot has got so many capabilities. It may become a part of your lifestyle. It is able to help in getting things done, staying informed about the latest news and events, checking your schedule and much more. It has also function to play music through Amazon Music, Pandora, iHeartRadio, Spotify, and TuneIn

The Amazon Echo Dot can make your life easier and innovative. It will give you all the benefits of the world in one place. It has got everything to meet all your expectations about a new level of high technologies. It's better to try it yourself and estimate all the advantages of this small device.

Chapter 1: Using Your Amazon Echo Dot (Second Generation)

The Amazon Echo Dot includes a lot of features for different users. One of the features is ability to control your home and also it performs many other mundane tasks to make your life more convenient.

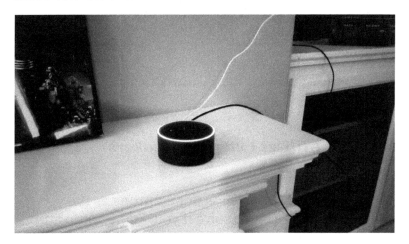

A new small version of Amazon Echo doesn't concede in the functionality. Besides, this innovative gadget is smaller and cheaper than the original. But the second generation Echo Dot is smaller than the first generation Echo Dot. This device is able to switch between wired and Bluetooth speakers by disabling Bluetooth connection, using your voice.

If you are a fan of Amazon Alexa user, this new product will exceed your expectations.
Don't worry that all of your devices will respond at once because this system is able to detect which Echo Dot you interact with your voice.

The new Echo Dot suggests a large variety of options and skills for any demanding user. You can find details on some of the functions that the Echo Dot performs and the description how to use them.

The Echo Dot Utilizes External Speakers

Despite the Echo Dot's speaker is not as strong as the original Echo but it is easy to solve if you connect it to an external speaker. You just need to connect a 3.5mm audio cord from the Amazon Echo Dot to an external speaker and it will make it possible the sound travelling from your Echo Dot from your external speaker.

To provide proper work of your Echo Dot, make sure it is on the right distance from the speaker. This distance should be at least 3 feet. Also check that your Amazon Echo Dot is more than 8 inches away from any other objects or walls.

The Echo Dot and the Voice Remote for the Amazon Echo

Comparing the previous versions of the Echo Dot and the Echo with the new second generation Echo Dot is absolutely compatible with the Voice Remote for the Amazon Echo. Using Bluetooth technology, it is able to connect to the Echo.

It is easy to use The Voice Remote as an optional addition to the Alexa-enabled devices and it enables them to speak to each other.
But only one remote can become the pair to one Echo device at once.
The Alexa app is necessary to provide the work of your remote with your Echo Dot. Using Alexa application, you should open your left navigation and select **Settings.** Then you should select the device that you want to connect with the remote. And then just select **Pair Device Remote** to pair your remote with the selected device.

To begin pairing with you device, just press the "Play" button on your remote for about 5 seconds. This procedure usually takes 40 seconds or longer to find and pair the device. When the setup is completed Alexa will inform you saying "Your remote has been paired."

The Echo Dot and Alexa Skills

Being a part of the Alexa family, the Echo Dot has got all the skills that the Alexa app can offer. It is able to perform everyday needs as a virtual assistant.

The Echo Dot has got the same functionality like the Amazon Echo. Its list of skills is long. Here are the most advertised ones:

Being that the Echo Dot can do everything the original Echo can, it has no shortage of functionality. Alexa offers a wide range of skills, the most advertised being:

- Uber

- 1-800-Flowers

- Domino's

- Lyft

- StubHub

- Capital One

Depending on your personal needs, you can choose which skills are helpful for you and add them through the Alexa app by selecting **Skills** from the left navigational panel.

The Alexa Family

The Alexa family is great as, beside the Echo Dot, it also included the original Amazon Echo, the first generation Echo Dot, and the Amazon Tap.

All these Amazon Alexa-enabled devices have some similarities but each of the products also has got some differences. Each device is meant for different type of user.

One of the portable Alexa devices is the Amazon Tap. Its main difference is that it is not "always on" that's why you have to say "Alexa" to wake it. You should also press the microphone (talk) button on the front of the Tap.

There are also other buttons: a power button, the Wi-Fi and Bluetooth buttons and dedicated playback buttons. The Amazon Tap doesn't have the traditional ring lighting but it has four indicator lights on the front. Unlike the Echo and the Echo Dot which have power adapters, the Tap has a non-removable, rechargeable battery.
The Tap set also includes a charging cradle and power adapter for said cradle. The Tap is also the only device which has Dolby audio.

The original Amazon Echo is larger than the Echo Dot and it has a mono speaker. The Echo has only two buttons which are the action button and mute button.

As for the other features, the Echo doesn't have the Bluetooth audio output, AUX audio input/output. The Echo is able to give strong, rich sound while playing music like two previous devices. In fact, the Echo Dot and Echo have much in common and they are able to perform the same functions.

Despite its smaller size, the Amazon Echo Dot can perform the same Alexa functions. Its sound is not so strong like the Echo has but you can connect it to an external speaker. One of the differences of the Echo Dot is that it has an AUX audio output and Bluetooth audio output and it is able to perform some functions that the Echo does not have. You will know about them in the next chapter.

Chapter 2: Connecting Your Echo Dot

To connect your Echo Dot you should put Echo Dot in a central location, at least eight inches from any windows and walls. Then take the power adapter which comes with Echo Dot and plug it into Echo Dot first, and then into a power outlet. You will see that the light ring on Echo Dot will first turn blue, and then proceed to orange. When you see the light turns orange, Alexa will greet the user.

Important Note: You should know that USB power adapters may not provide enough power for functionality of Echo Dot.

1. **Connect Echo Dot to a Wi-Fi network.**

Then you have to follow the instructions in the Alexa App and connect Echo Dot to a Wi-Fi network.

Tips:

- If the process doesn't start automatically, press and hold the **Action** button on Echo Dot for a while. Then open the Alexa app and find

Settings > Set up a new device.

- If Echo Dot doesn't connect to the Wi-Fi network you should restart Amazon Echo Dot by unplugging and re-plugging the device one more time.
  If you still have trouble you should reset Echo Dot to the factory settings and follow the set up steps again.
- You can learn more information here: <u>Reset Your Echo Device</u>.

2. Follow the following steps: select your Wi-Fi network and enter the network password (if required). If your Wi-Fi network isn't listed, you should scroll down and select **Add a Network** (for hidden networks) or **Rescan**.

   MAC address: In case if you need to add your Alexa device to your router's list of approved devices, you should scroll down on that screen and you will see the MAC address.

   Optional: you should save your Wi-Fi password to Amazon. Remember that any Wi-Fi passwords saved during setup can automatically appear when you connect a new

Alexa device to the same Wi-Fi network. The system also remembers the password if you switch between saved Wi-Fi networks.

1. Then select **Connect**. After your device is connected to your Wi-Fi network, a confirmation message appears in the app. You're now ready to use Alexa.

3. **Talking to Alexa.**

Now we can get started as the Echo device is ready to perform your orders. Just say the "wake word" and then speak in a normal manner to Alexa. The Echo Dot normally responds to the wake word "Alexa" by default, but you can change the wake word at any time. Using the Alexa app, go to Settings, select correct Echo device, and then choose **Wake word**.

Once you've installed the Alexa app, open it and follow the instructions in the app or on the website (if using a browser to complete set up) to make sure you've correctly completed the setup of the Echo Dot. It is necessary to enable the local Wi-Fi network information to be entered by the user and Echo Dot can connect to the internet. This is normal if

Amazon asks you for account login information. The app-based process will be described in details in this book. Besides, Alexa App web-based set up process is very similar to the app-based process. You should open the Alexa app on a mobile device or swipe to open the left menu and touch the three horizontal lines in the upper left corner and open the menu.

Then tap the Settings button, then you will see the list of available devices to load. Once this list has been loaded completely, select the Echo Dot device from the menu.

Then tap the Update Wi-Fi button.

Your Echo Device Doesn't Connect to the Wi-Fi Network.

To ensure the right work of your Amazon Dot, check your Wi-Fi network that it meets the standards of dual-band Wi-Fi (2.4 GHz/5 GHz) networks that use the 802.11a/b/g/n.

The current status of your Wi-Fi network is showed by the power LED on your Echo. You can place the power LED near the power adapter port on the device.

Power LED State	Description
Solid white light	Echo device is connected to your Wi-Fi network
Solid orange light	Echo device is not connected to your Wi-Fi network
Blinking orange light	Echo device is connected to your Wi-Fi network, but it can't access the Alexa Voice Service.

In case if you have troubles with starting Echo, try to following actions:

➤ Restart your Wi-Fi network again.

➢ Make sure you enter the right network password (if required). If you see a lock icon, it means that a network password is required. This password is not your Amazon account password.

➢ you should also verify if other devices, such as tablets or mobile phones can connect to your network. If not, the problem may be with your Wi-Fi network. To solve this problem, you should contact your Internet service provider, network administrator, or the person who set up your network. They should help you with it.

➢ You should update the firmware for your router or modem hardware.

➢ In case if you saved your Wi-Fi password to Amazon, but you decided to change it, you need to re-enter your new Wi-Fi password to connect again.

➢ In some situations, by default, your router may use both WPA+WPA2 for security. You can solve this problem with connection if you switch the router security type to either WPA or WPA2 only. If the router also has an option to set the type of encryption, you should set it only to AES.

Another tip is to reduce Wi-Fi congestion

- ➢ You may have inconsistent Wi-Fi performance when you have multiple devices on your Wi-Fi network.
- ➢ You should turn off devices that you aren't using to free up bandwidth on your network.
- ➢ You should move your device closer to your router and modem if it's blocked by an object.
- ➢ You should make sure that there are no other sources of possible interference, such as microwave ovens or baby monitors.
- ➢ **Optional:** You can connect to your router's 5 GHz Wi-Fi frequency band (if it's available). Many Wi-Fi devices only connect to the 2.4 GHz band. If you have many devices that use this band on your network, your network speed may be slower. But you can connect to the less congested 5 GHz band to get better range and less interference.

Connecting to a Wi-Fi Hotspot

Wi-Fi hotspot is useful when you are not at home or near a public Wi-Fi network. You should just connect your Echo Dot to a Wi-Fi hotspot on your mobile device.

You should also know some information before installing it on your mobile device:

- Your Echo Dot will need latest software update (3389 or higher). The latest version for your Echo or Echo Dot (First Generation) is 4148 and for Echo Dot (Second Generation) is 5.5.0.1. After downloading and installing this update ESP

(Echo Spatial Perception) technology your Echo Dot will be able to understand better which one must answer your question or request.

- The other feature that you need is a cellular service plan that supports Wi-Fi hotspots

- You will also need the Alexa app that your mobile device is able to support (iOS, Android)

Have you got the most recent software version?

In case if you set up the option to connect your Dot to a mobile hotspot for the first time it may be not available. If it is not for the first time then you should connect your Echo Dot to your home Wi-Fi network and to download and install the recent software update which enables this feature. When you connect to a Wi-Fi network Alexa updates are automatically downloaded. The latest updates are necessary to fix issues from previous updates, to add new Alexa features and to improve performance.

After opening the left navigation panel and selecting **Settings** you can determine the current software version in the Alexa app. Then you should highlight your device and scroll down until you see ***Device Software Version***.

You should make sure your device is on and Wi-Fi is active to be able to install the latest version. Try to avoid saying anything to your device while the update is running. When light ring on your device turns blue that means it is ready to install. It may take about 15 minutes to complete the installation, depending on your Wi-Fi network.

Note: If you have some issues with the software updates after downloading you should restart your device. You should unplug the power adaptor from the back of the Echo and then plug it back in. When you have done restarting your device, you should wait for the update to install again.

Connecting Your Echo Dot to a Wi-Fi Hotspot:

1. Navigate in the **Settings** menu on your mobile device, then search for Wi-Fi hotspot option, copy the network name and the password for your hotspot.
2. Then you should open the left navigation panel in the Alexa app and select **Settings**.
3. The next step is to locate and select your Echo Dot and then select **Update Wi-Fi**.
4. Then you should press and hold the **Action** button on your Echo Dot for a few seconds. When the light ring turns orange that means your mobile device connects to your Echo Dot and a list of available Wi-Fi networks is available.

   Note: You can get question from Alexa to connect manually your device to Echo Dot through your Wi-Fi settings.
5. Then you should scroll down and select **Use this device as a Wi-Fi hotspot**.
6. Then you should select **Start**.
7. You should enter the Wi-Fi hotspot network name and the password that you copied from the **Settings** menu on your mobile device. If you cannot paste the information you should be sure to enter the network information the same as it is shown on your mobile device. Otherwise, your Echo Dot won't be able to connect to your Wi-Fi hotspot.
8. Then you should navigate to your mobile device's **Settings** menu and turn on your Wi-Fi hotspot. The Echo Dot will find for your Wi-Fi hotspot and connect. Then Alexa will approve a successful connection.

Important: It's necessary to know when you use your mobile device as a Wi-Fi hotspot your Dot usually uses the device's data connection. That's why your service provider may apply additional charges. It depends on your current data plan. You should contact your service provider if you have any questions about data usage when you connect your Amazon Echo Dot to your Wi-Fi hotspot.

Chapter 3: Advanced Functions and Advanced Settings of the Amazon Echo Dot

Functions, Fun, and Advanced Settings on Your Echo Dot

In this chapter you will know about some functions that Echo Dot can perform. Here you will also read about advanced settings the device has. This chapter contains all necessary information you need to know about functions of your Echo Dot.

Music and Media with Your Amazon Echo

The Amazon Echo Dot is famous for its option of listening to music and books. It makes appealing for a great number of users as the Echo Dot has connection with third-party applications and subscription services.

Even you do not have a music subscription you are able to connect the Dot to their library using Alexa.

Listening to Music on Your Alexa Device

The Amazon Echo Dot offers such a great variety of options: listening to podcasts, stream music, audiobooks and adding your music library on Amazon from iTunes, Google Play, and many others.

You can also ask Alexa to stream music from different subscription services. The services may have free and paid music subscriptions.

Here are the following subscription services:

- Amazon Music

- Audible

- iHeartRadio

- Prime Music

- Amazon Music Unlimited

- Spotify Premium

- TuneIn

Upload Music to Your Library

If you want to play your personal music library you should use Amazon Music for PC or Mac to be able to upload your songs into "My Music" section on Amazon. You can upload 250 songs for free but if you want to add more song you must have an Amazon Music Subscription.

Note: If you have free account you cannot buy more than 250 songs via the Digital Music Store for free.

Third-Party Music Services

You can get access to third-party music services by linking your music service account within Alexa. To provide this you should select **Music & Books** from the navigation panel within the app and select the streaming service you want. Once you have selected the desired streaming service you should select **Link Account to Alexa** and sign in with your credentials. Then you will be able to use Alexa with the desired service.

Audible and Kindle Unlimited

It's also possible to use your Echo Dot stream audiobooks and other media. Audible and Kindle can be used with the Dot. You will be able to read newspaper and magazine audio subscriptions, notes, bookmarks and narration speed controls.

Here are some commands that you can use:

- *"Play [title of work] from Audible."*

- *"Stop reading the book in [60] minutes."*

- *"Play the book, [Huckleberry Finn]."*

LENDING LIBRARY

Alexa can also be helpful for reading items from Amazon Kindle. The books that you have purchased from the Kindle store, the items shared within your Family Library or borrowed from Kindle Unlimited or Kindle Owners' Lending Library are included in eligible books.

For this moment, Alexa is not able to support comics, graphic novels, or narration speed control.

Here are simple commands for Amazon Kindle:

- *"Read my book, [book title]."*

- *"Read my Kindle Book."*

Music Unlimited for Echo Devices

You can listen to a great variety of music on your Echo Dot device if you have the Amazon Music subscription.

You can buy your Amazon Music Unlimited for Echo Subscription with the help of Alexa and your Echo Dot. If you have never had a music subscription, you can get free trial via voice commands.

You should know that the free trial takes $1for your account and it will be removed within 72 hours.

You should say "Sign up for Amazon Music Unlimited" to complete the signing up for a music subscription via Alexa. And Alexa will help you with this procedure.

Flash Briefings

You can get updates from popular broadcasters, the latest headlines from the Associated Press and weather information with the help of flash briefing.

But first you have to customize your settings within the Alexa app. You can have these things customized: shows, weather updates, headlines. It is also possible to edit the order in which the program plays in your flash briefings.

You can view more flash briefing content if you use the "Get More Flash Briefing Content". You also have such option when Alexa has read the flash brief you can also read the full stories as the link will appear in your Alexa application.

Here are simple commands for your Flash Briefing:

- *"What's new?"*

- *"What's my flash briefing?"*

Sports Updates

You can get the results of the latest scores and game information for your teams by asking Alexa. But first you have to set up them in the Alexa app to enable this feature.

Just select **Settings** > **Sports Update** and add your sport teams from the Alexa app. Then you should enter the name of your favourite sports team into the search field and you will see the suggestions of the team names.

So next time, when you want to hear your sports updates, tell Alexa *"Give me my Sports Update"*.

Weather Forecast

If you need to know weather forecast every day, your Echo Dot can help you with it. It is able to give local weather forecasts as well as the weather in any city of U.S. You should just add your address in the Alexa app to provide more accurate forecast.

You can easily edit the information from the Alexa settings menu and change your location.

Using the Alexa app, you can get a seven-day forecast when you ask Alexa about the weather. Usually Alexa takes the information from AccuWeather to provide the weather forecast.

Here is the list of phrases you can use to know your weather forecast:

- What's the weather today?
- What's the weather for tomorrow?
- What's the weather for this weekend?

Traffic Requests

If you want to set up traffic updates in Alexa, first, you must have a travel route set within the app. Your starting location is usually associated with the address you have entered in your Amazon account.

You can update your traffic conditions according to your desired route and its duration with the help of Alexa. To provide updates just select **Settings** >

Traffic from your Alexa app and update "from" and "to" address.

Here are the phrases to ask Alexa about traffic updates:

- *"How is traffic?"*
- *"What's my commute?"*

Nearby Locations

If you don't know which restaurant to choose tonight or where to do shopping in your area your Amazon Echo Dot will find it for you. In order to provide this Alexa usually uses your device location in combination with Yelp.

Alexa is ready to help you with any searches to find exactly what you need. Your Amazon Echo Dot is able to find top-rated businesses, business hours and phone numbers, different business types and to get the addresses of nearby business.

Movie Showtimes

Alexa is also able to find movies and movie showtimes as your address is already set up in the Alexa app. You need to use your cell phone, Alexa will do it for you. While searching for specific theatres and movies Alexa uses IMDb.

Using your Dot you are able to find out what movies are playing near you, movies playing in other cities as well as specific showtimes. You can also be more specific with your requests by asking to find specific showtimes at a specific theater.

Ask Alexa

Echo Dot is able to answer almost all your question concerning world, people, dates, history, geography, trivia and many others. Alexa can even do some simple calculations, spell words or define them.

Here are useful phrases:

- *"Who is [person name]?"*

- *"Who starred in the TV Show [title]?"*

- *"When is [holiday]?"*

- *"Who starred in the Movie [title]?"*

Productivity

This amazing device is able to become a great assistant for a person who needs planning, making to-do lists, updating his calendars. Amazon Echo Dot is a little organizer which is able to wake you up, to give updates on the nearest events and necessary tasks, and many other options.

Timers and Alarms

Alexa can also help with setting multiple timers or alarms. You can set up timers and alarms to 24 hours ahead of time.

If you have already set up alarm with your voice you can edit it inside the Alexa app. Besides, you can make new alarms, turn them on or off, using the Alexs app.

The Alexa app can perform three functionalities. You can change your alarm volume, alarm sound or delete an alarm Here are the voice commands for alarms:

- *"Set a repeating alarm for [day of week] at [time]."*

- *"Wake me up at [time]."*

- *"What alarms do I have?"*

You can get a great variety of functionality with timers. But you can pause, resume your timer or change your timer volume only by using the Alexa app.

You should remember that you cannot change timer's volume using the device volume as they work independently.

Here is the list of voice commands that you can use with timers:

- *"Set the timer for [time]."*

- *"Set a timer for [x amount of time]."*

Manage Lists

If you have a great list of important tasks every day then Amazon Echo Dot is ready to help you with it. You should know that each list must not exceed 100 items and each item must not contain more than 256 characters.

You can open your shopping and to-do lists through the Alexa app, the Amazon app and the Alexa Shopping list. Alexa is also able to add some item to your shopping or to-do list and review it when you use your Echo Dot.

Besides, Alexa can link the third-party list services. Let's see this option in details.

Linking Third-Party List Services to Your Echo Dot

This option is useful as it helps to manage tasks and things that you need to remember. Your Echo Dot should be used with third-party list services to provide this option.

If you want to activate this option you should link the service in the Alexa app. So go to the **Settings** > **Lists** and select **Link** to see the desired list service. Then you should enter your login or create a new account. You can use the screen prompts to complete your setup.

Adding or Reviewing Calendar Events

Your Dot can also help you if you want to add or review events in your Google Calendar. But, first, you have to link your Google Calendar within the Alexa app to start using the calendar features.

To activate this option, go to **Settings** > **Calendar** and select **Google Calendar**. Then select **Link Google Calendar Account** to link your active Google calendar.

Then you should make sure that you have selected the proper calendar to be able to add events to your calendar.

Here are the phrases for managing your calendar:

- *"What's on my calendar on [day]?"*

- *"When is my next event?"*

- *"Add [event] to my calendar for [day] at [time]."*

Using Voicecast to Send Content

You can also use your Echo Dot to send details about news, weather and other things to your Fire tablet. You just need to turn on Automatic Voicecast and you will be able to send the content to your Fire tablet automatically.

You will see the notification on the lock screen of the tablet that the content has been sent to your Fire tablet. When you unlock the device you will see the notification in the Quick Settings menu of your Fire tablet.

Voicecast also include a lot of Alexa features such as:

- Music

- Questions and answers

- Flash Briefing

- Lists

- Weather

- Timer and alarms

- Wikipedia

- Help

  If you want to ask Alexa about something, simply say *"Send that to [device name]"* or *"Show this on my Fire tablet"*.

Shopping and Placing Orders with Alexa

You can also do particular shopping using your Echo Dot. You can buy music, order an Alexa device, or place orders using Alexa.

When you need to make a purchase Alexa is able to search through various purchase options which include:

- Your order history: You can order only Prime-eligible items using Alexa.
- Prime-eligible items: They include items which are eligible for delivery by Prime now.

- Amazon's Choice: You can choose some items which has high rating and good price with Prime shipping.

Purchasing with Alexa is easy as she usually tells the item name and price before purchasing. She can also provide additional shipping information in case the purchase will not be delivered through Amazon Prime. Then Alexa will ask you either to confirm or cancel the order.

Alexa also have additional options which make shopping on Amazon more convenient. She is able to add items to your cart, add items to an Alexa Shopping list or you can ask for more information if the item cannot be found or you cannot complete the purchase.

You should also set up some requirements on your Amazon account to be able to place an order using your Alexa device.

If you want to make an order from the Digital Music Store you should have annual Prime Membership. You must have Amazon account and a payment method must be set up in 1-click settings. The same requirements are for purchasing physical products.

You can navigate your shopping setting through the Alexa app. You can turn off voice purchasing or require a confirmation code before every order.

Here are the commands for purchasing Prime-eligible items:

- *"Order a [item name]."* If Alexa has found the product you should say yes/no to confirm.

- *"Reorder [item name]."* If Alexa has found the product you should say yes/no to confirm.

- *"Add [item name] to my cart."* Alexa will add an item to your cart on Amazon.

- *"Cancel my order."* Alexa will cancel an order immediately.

If you purchase some music maybe you will need a confirmation code before initiating a purchase. This will prevent from purchasing music on your account by someone else.

You should use the following commands to buy music:

- *"Shop for the song [song name]."*

- *"Shop for the album [album name]."*

- *"Buy this [song]." You can use* this command if some song is playing on an Amazon-supported station.

Tracking Orders with Your Echo Dot

Using your Echo Dot, you can also track your orders via Alexa. If you have more than one active order, Alexa will give you information about the order with a delivery date that is closest to the current date

Here are the phrases to track your orders:

- *"Where is my stuff?"* or *"Track my order"*

After these phrases Alexa will give you information about your orders.

Amazon Echo Dot also can serve as a hub for your home control. It is able to control your lights, different switches around your home, your thermostat, such items like Phillips, Hive, or Hue devices. You will get to know how to control your smart home in the following chapters.

Changing the Wake Word

Normally the Echo Dot recognizes the word "Alexa" as the wake word but you can change this word to the word "Amazon" if you want using the Alexa app. You should open the Alexa app, swipe open, then look at the left-hand menu, open the **Settings** section, tap on the Echo Dot in the device list. Then you should select the **Wake word option** and here you can change it between the words "Alexa" and "Amazon." If you change the wake word for Dot, it may standby for a while as it needs reconfiguration to recognize the new word.

Reset to Factory Defaults

In case if you have troubles while your Echo Dot listen or performs some tasks you should try resetting it. It happens with any device from time to time. Even if it has been working for a short time the device needs full resetting to work properly.

You will need a paperclip to reset the Echo Dot. Follow these steps: turn the Echo Dot upside down and insert the paperclip into the small hole that is labeled as RESET and press the reset button. Then hold the button for 10–20 seconds. You will see that the light ring will turn on, turn off and then turn on again before beginning the setup of Echo Dot like when it was first received.

Fun Phrases to Try Out with Alexa

Here is the list of funny phrases you can try for your Echo Dot or any device with Alexa. There are even more phrases that Amazon Alexa development team has put into Alexa. Check them out:

Alexa, who's your daddy?

Alexa, I am your father.

Alexa, all your base are belong to us.

Alexa, Romeo, Romeo wherefore art thou Romeo?

Alexa, beam me up.

Alexa, how many roads must a man walk down?

Alexa, who lives in a pineapple under the sea?

Alexa, what is the meaning of life?

Alexa, what is the loneliest number?

Alexa, how much is that doggie in the window?

Alexa, define rock, paper, scissors, lizard, Spock.

Alexa, how much wood can a woodchuck chuck if a woodchuck could chuck wood?

Alexa, Earl Grey. Hot. (or Alexa, tea. Earl Grey. Hot.)

Alexa, what does the Earth weigh?

Alexa, when is the end of the world?

Alexa, make me a sandwich.

Alexa, do you have a boyfriend?

Alexa, do you want to build a snowman?

Alexa, do you really want to hurt me?

Alexa, what is the best tablet?

Alexa, which comes first: the chicken or the egg?

Alexa, may the force be with you.

Alexa, what is your favorite color?

Alexa, who won best actor Oscar in 1973?

Alexa, what is your quest?

Alexa, do aliens exist?

Alexa, how many licks does it take to get to the center of a Tootsie pop?

Alexa, what are you going to do today?

Alexa, where do you live?

Alexa, what is the airspeed velocity of an unladen swallow?

Alexa, where do babies come from?

Alexa, what is love?

Alexa, who is the real Slim Shady?

Alexa, who let the dogs out?

Alexa, open the pod bay doors.

Chapter 4: The Echo/Echo Dot Voice Remote

The official remote is necessary for the Echo and Echo Dot to connect the devices via Bluetooth. The remote is 5.5 inches long and 1.5 inches wide. When you are far away from Alexa or the room is too noisy you can use the integrated microphone in the remote. The remote can be used from any room in your house and also on the distance up to 100+ feet away. The buttons of remote are able to move to the next or previous track, play or pause, and control the volume of the device(s). The remote is able to work with only one Echo device at a time and it is not compatible with the Amazon Tap or the Fire TV.

The remote uses 2 AAA which are available with the setup right out of the box. Later you will need to change them but it may be a little difficult for you to remove the battery cover to replace the batteries. You should follow these steps to remove the battery cover easily: hold the remote face down in the palm of your hand with the top pointed away from you. Then you should find the battery cover tab, indicated by that is the inside of an equal sign, and using something hard, but not sharp, press down on the tab while also pulling the bottom of the cover up. It is not so difficult as it seems for the first time.

You can get the instructions from the Alexa app in the **Settings** menu option if they are not included with the remote. You should select **Pair device remote** and the device that you want to pair it with. Then it will ask you to press and hold the play button on the remote for a few seconds until it's been detected. Once it's detected you are able to use it.

If you need to activate the voice control you should press and hold the mic button while you speak. In this case means you don't need to use your chosen wake word (Alexa, Amazon, or Echo) with the remote. While holding the mic button, just say your command *"Turn on kitchen"* and depending on the skill you've setup, the kitchen lights will be turned on. You should know that you will need to hold the mic button for the whole command to be heard and understood. If you just press and release while speaking you will not manage to activate the voice control.

As you know, you can enable the remote only for one device at a time. But if you would like to pair a second remote to be able to have one in different parts of the house, you should go to the Alexa app and choose **Settings** > **Echo** > **Bluetooth** > **Pair a new device.**

When the pair process gets started, you should press the play button on the second remote for about 5 seconds until you see it as an *Unknown Device* in the device list. When you connect the Echo to it, it seems like pairing another Bluetooth speaker, but this is the second remote. You will not see the second remote anywhere in the Bluetooth device list but both remotes will then work with that Echo device. That means you are able to use remotes with one Echo device or pair each remote with its own Echo device.

When you are in a noisy room or the volume is loud Alexa may not be able to hear and understand what you say. You can use the remote to pause or stop the music or loud volume. When it is quiet enough you can control the device by speaking to it.

It is necessary to know that the remote is included in the package deal with the first generation Echo and Echo Dot for Amazon Prime members, but it does not come with the second generation Echo Dot. Also, when you purchased as the package the remote came with a magnetic holster. But now it is not included when you purchase it separately that is required.

Chapter 5: Second Generation Amazon Echo Dot as a Smart Home

The Amazon Echo Dot has got much more functions that you can imagine. It is able to make your life more convenient and smarter. The Echo Dot is a perfect device that can make the Home Automation Process. You can purchase these smart options with the Dot from Amazon.com.

Here are some helpful tips how you can use your Amazon Echo Dot to make your home smarter.

Using Your Amazon Dot with the Bose Soundlink Mini II

You can use the Echo Dot with a great variety of Bluetooth speakers. One of the options for pairing with the device is the Bose Soundlink Mini II. It is able to play up for up to 10 hours on a full charge. You can easily go through the Bluetooth connection process with the help of the voice prompts on the device.

You should connect the Echo Dot via Bluetooth or through the 3.5mm stereo cable. Then you should follow the described instructions to pair via Bluetooth.

1. First, place your Bose Soundlink Mini II in pairing mode.

2. Select **Settings** within the Alexa app on your phone or tablet.

3. Then select **Bluetooth** > **Pair a New Device** and your Dot will enter pairing mode. You will see Bose speaker in the list of devices when it is found. Then select your speaker.

4. When you have successfully connected your speaker, Alexa will give you confirmation. After this moment you can connect and disconnect from your speaker just using your voice.

Using Your Amazon Dot with the Phillips Hue Starter Kit

You can easily control your home lighting after pairing the Amazon Dot with the Phillips Hue Starter kit. As you know, the starter kit comes with a bridge and two bulbs, but the bridge can wirelessly connect to up to 50 lights. The two bulbs included in this kit are 800 lumens comparing with the first generation kit with the bulbs of 600 lumens.

The bridge enables you to control lighting from your device or your Echo Dot by using Alexa. It is easy to set up your Phillips lighting with Alexa. Follow these steps:

1. Open the Alexa app on your smart device and go to **Settings**.

2. Then open **Connected Home** from Settings in the account section. Then choose **Discover Devices** in the device section from there.

3. Then press the button on your Phillips Hue Bridge to enable connection. You should see your bulbs in the device section. In this section you can create groups which represent the rooms where you can control the lighting. Now you can use your lights.

Note: If you want to do more than brighten and dim your lights you should authorize Alexa to work with your IFTTT account. After this you will be able to create triggers and specific phrases to control lighting functions.

Using Your Amazon Dot with the TP-Link Smart Plug

Another way that enables you to control your home is the TP-Link Smart plug. You will be able to control your device from any location using the TP-Link Kasa App, schedule the automation of electronics if necessary, and utilize "Away Mode." Using Away Mode you can   turn your devices on and off at different time to give the illusion that you are at home when you are away.

The TP-Link also enables you to control the television or whatever device is plugged into it. It is also easy to set up this function. Follow the next instructions to make sure you have set up your TP- Link Smart Plug properly.

1. Select **Smart Home** from the Alexa app. This is the setup you will need to add this skill to the Smart Home area. Then you should search for**TP-Link Kasa**.

2. Then select **Enable skill** when you have located the skill and log into your TP-Link account.
3. To provide proper work for your device with the Echo Dot turn on the **Remote Control** function from the Kasa app. To enable this function simply go into your desired device > Select the **Settings** icon > under **Device Controls**, select **Remote Control**.

4. Then you should place Alexa in **Discover Mode** and say "*Alexa discover devices.*" Alexa will search for your Smart Plug. When it completes the search you will be able to control the desired device with your voice.

Using Your Amazon Dot with the ecobee3 Smart Thermostat

You should know you will never have to walk to the thermostat again if you purchase the Amazon Echo Dot in conjunction with the ecobee3 Smart Thermostat.

The ecobee3 Smart Thermostat works on your comfort and it is able to detect if the rooms are occupied or when nobody is at home.

Follow these instructions to connect your Dot to your ecobee3.

1. First, open your Alexa app and navigate to the **Settings**.
2. Select **Connected Home** from the settings. Then scroll until you see **Device Links** and select **Link with ecobee**.

3. Then you will be asked to log into your ecobee account and authorize ecobee with your device.

4. The notification ***Unlink the ecobee*** will appear when the device has been linked.

The only way that can be used is linking these items with your Amazon Echo Dot (Second Generation). It gives a great variety of other functionality.

Here is the list of other featured brands which cooperate with the Amazon Echo Dot:

It offers a plethora of other functionality. Other featured brands which perform with the Amazon Echo Dot include:

- Insteon

- Wink

- Samsung SmartThings

- WeMo

- Honeywell

Smart Home Device Groups

You can also create a device group within the Alexa application to control multiple smart home devices all at once. Here are the instructions if you want to create a smart home group:

1. Locate **Smart Home** from your left navigation panel in the Alexa app

2. Then select **Groups** > **Create Groups.**

3. Then you should enter your desired group name. The rooms names are used to give your group a recognizable name

4. Then select the devices in which you prefer to add to this group and select **Add** when you have completed.

After creating your groups in the Alexa app you will be able to use commands via Alexa with it. You may also need to say Alexa to "*Open [skill name]*" for some skills before your request can be recognized.

Here are some commands that you can use with your smart home devices:

- *"Turn on [Smart Device Name or group]."*

- *"Set my living room fan to [#]%."*

- *"Set [Group Name] to [#]%."*

You can manage your device scene through the desired device's companion application. You can see the scene names in the Smart Home section of the Alexa application.

Chapter 6: IFTTT and Amazon Echo Dot

IFTTT is a short abbreviation from 'If This, Then That'. This free web-based service IFTTT gives possibility to connect different applications to create the chains of conditional statements which are called "Recipes". These "Recipes" are step-by-step commands which are used to improve your Alexa experience. It's an automation service that enables to connect the majority of your things through the Internet. You can configure the settings using your mobile device and also using IFTTT website.

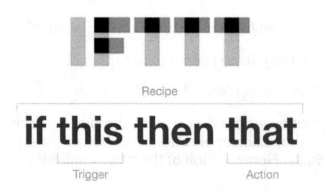

IFTT is a mobile application and a website that works with Phillips Hue systems, Alexa, and many other applications. If you have Smart Home items IFTTT is able to automate everything from it to simple notifications on your phone.

You should use IFTTT application with Alexa to setup recipes that you can use with the following applications:

- Phillips Hue

- Google Drive

- Todoist

- GMail

- Evernote

- Google Calendar

- Nest

- Harmony

IFTTT is able to give endless opportunities to empower your Echo Dot. You should also know that all IFTTT connections can be uploaded through a mobile device as well as online.

You can the popularity of your recipe by checking the number of users who have enabled that recipe for their Alexa device. The number of these users is at the bottom of the recipe card next to the person icon. While using IFTTT online you can see how many people have saved some recipes. You can understand if this recipe is good by the number of people who have saved it.

There is an 'Activity Log' under the notifications selection button that shows when the recipe was run. So you can receive alerts when the recipe is run.

Using the "My Applets" screen you can monitor your applets or actions activity as a whole. If you select 'All' or 'Activity' you will see all of the applets or actions that you have turned configured in the past. It will also show you when each of your applets was created and when, if any, were turned off. You can also see when any services were connected to your account.

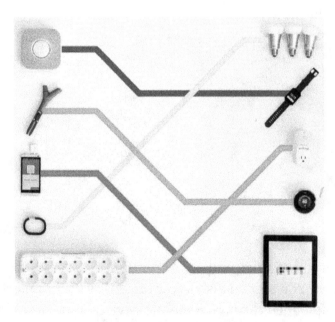

Connecting to the Alexa channel in IFTTT

First of all you have to connect to the IFTTT Alexa channel to be able to stay current with all of the preset options for the Alexa and connect to the options available to you. You should follow these instructions:

1. Go to IFTTT online or on your mobile application and search for "Amazon Alexa"
2. When you have found it you should select "Connect" button.
3. Then you will have to enter your Amazon account login information.
4. Then you must select "Okay" to give IFTTT Permission to access your Amazon account.
5.
6. Then you will receive the confirmation that you are successfully connected to the IFTTT channel.

And now you can create and use recipes. You can also test Alexa & IFTTT setup with Phillips Hue, your cellular device and your Google Calendar.

How to connect the Echo Dot with IFTTT

It's easy to connect your Echo Dot to different compatible functions because IFTTT has an Amazon Alexa Channel where you can link it.

In order to connect you Dot to IFTTT you should follow these instructions below:

1. Find the Alexa Channel page from your IFTTT application and select the **Connect** button to start the setup.
2. Then you will be prompted to sign into your Amazon account and to share some additional information with IFTTT that is associated with your Echo Dot. You should select *I Agree* to move forward. Then your account will be connected with Amazon
3. Then you will see a list of predefined recipes which are available for Alexa and choose the function you want. Then select *Turn On*. After this moment your selected action will be performed by IFTTT.

4. When you select a pre-defined recipe you are able to configure that recipe or leave it as it is. You should make sure that you are reading the configuration just to know how to trigger events with Alexa.

   You will be shown the trigger was ran and given the option to "check now" on each of your selected actions. It is necessary to determine if the trigger is working.

The Echo Dot, IFTTT and Your Smart Home

IFTTT play the role of a central hub which helps to create and to use recipes to run your smart home with. The web-based service IFTTT and Alexa can work with such applications like SmartThings, Phillips Hue, and Harmony.

This service allows Alexa to perform the following actions: changing the light color, toggling device power, turning lights on and locking doors.

Using the IFTTT dashboard, you can create new recipes by selecting the *Create New Recipe* link. The other way is to search for the application in which you can choose to connect the necessary recipe to.

1. When you've selected the action or the application you should proceed to choose a trigger from the variety you can see.
2. The next action is to complete the trigger field.
3. Then you should choose your action channel. If you are connecting the light bulbs you should select the action channel for this product.
4. The next step is to choose the action associated to it. If you have chosen the action with light bulbs, it may be "turn lights on," "turn lights off," or many other options such as fading in, color options, etc.

5. Then you will be able to use your trigger.

Find your phone

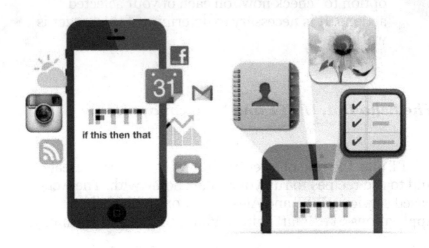

The following instructions concern how to configure Alexa to find your phone:

1. You should search 'Amazon Alexa' within the IFTTT application and then you will be shown a list of the already preset Alexa functions.
2. Then you should select "Tell Alexa to find my phone" from the list of pre-set recipes.
3. Then tap the "Turn On" button to get started with setup.
4. You will also be prompted to accept the permissions needed for the trigger to function correctly.
5. After you have accepted the permissions you should enter a phone number. When the "Send Pin" button is selected this number will be called. This pin will also be used to verify the call information that will be used when Alexa

gets instructions to find the device.

6. When you have entered your call information you will receive a confirmation that the phone call has been selected.

After configuration this recipe when you need to find your phone you tell Alexa to find your phone. And then you will be receive a call with a default message of, "Alexa attempted to find your phone on [trigger date]". It is a customizable call message and it may be changed based according to your preferences.

Syncing Alexa To Do List to Your Google Calendar

You can connect a lot of devices with your Echo Dot using IFTTT. The other function for IFTTT and Alexa is syncing your Alexa To – Do list with your Google Calendar.

1. You should search 'Amazon Alexa' within the IFTTT application and then you will be shown a list of the already preset Alexa functions.

2. You should select "Automatically sync Alexa to-dos to your Google calendar" from the list of pre-set recipes.
3. Then you should select 'OK' to give IFTTT the needed permissions to access to Google Calendar.
4. In order to connect your Google Account with IFTTT you should select the Google Account you would like to use with your Alexa to do list and select 'Allow'.
5. Now Alexa is connected to your Google account through IFTTT and it will automatically sync your to do list items with the calendar.

Alexa can also be connected to outside devices like Bluetooth speakers except syncing Alexa to applications and items in your phone, or Smart home devices.

Alexa & Phillips Hue Lighting

Alexa is able to work with many smart home devices. And one of these devices is Phillips Hue Lighting. You can also add voice commands to your lighting system using Alexa and IFTTT.

The following instructions should help you not only setting

up IFTTT, Alexa and Hue lighting, but they will teach you how to successfully connect your hue with trigger commands. Follow these steps:

1. You should search 'Amazon Alexa' within the IFTTT application. Then you will be shown a list of the already preset Alexa functions.
2. Then you should select "Tell Alexa to start the party and put your Hue lights on a color loop " from the list of pre-set recipes.
3. Then select 'OK' to give IFTTT the needed permissions to access to Phillips Hue.
4. Then you will be prompted to log into your Hue Account or to create a new one.
5. You will also receive a notification that your mobile device may now be used to control you Hue lighting.
6. Then you will be sent back to the IFTTT application to configure the settings for your command.
7. You are also able to change the trigger phrase for the recipe within the configurations and select which lights will function on command.
8. When you have completed your desired configurations you should select the check mark.

You cannot imagine how many activities Alexa is able to perform with Hue Lights. It is able to change the lighting based on song. Alexa can also change the lights when items are added to the to do list and even make your lights blink when your timer hits zero.

Custom IFTTT Recipes

Except using the preset recipes as listed above you are also able to create recipes from scratch. You should select "Applet Maker" from within the Amazon Alexa channel and you can start creating your own recipes. You can see the button listed under "Try making your own Applet from scratch".

1. When the next screen loads you should select the '+' sign next to the word "this".
2. Then choose Amazon Alexa as your trigger service.
3. There is a list of triggers that you may use based on the functions of Alexa which is on the next page.
4. When you have chosen your trigger then you will be brought back the previous "If this then that" screen or asked to configure the specific item selected.
5. Now you should see the icon for your If function on the applet maker screen. If it is not there, you should repeat steps 1-4.
6. Then select the '+' sign next to the word 'that' to create the action for your recipe.
7. You will see the list of services offered through the IFTTT app once again. You should select the service for your desired action.
8. Then you should complete the configuration of the action, based on the chosen service. When the action

is complete, you should finish your action by selecting the check mark, in the top right hand corner of the screen.

9. When your recipe is complete you will see a summary of your new action. Then select 'Finish' if you are satisfied with the result.

10. Then you will receive a notification message that your new action will be set to 'On'.

In case you have forgotten about recipe you can just select "Check Now" to make sure it is set up correctly.

One of the main functions of IFTTT is its ability to chain multiple recipes together in one bundle. It enables you to give Alexa a command and trigger multiple actions.

IFTT is a necessary tool for your Amazon Echo Dot to automate and control your everyday tasks. If it seems hard to configure your recipes for the first time, soon you will get used to customizing your own recipes and instructions.

Chapter 7: How to Overcome the Disadvantages of the Echo Dot

As you know, every item has its advantages and disadvantages. Amazon Echo Dot (Second Generation) can perform a lot of necessary functions despite its small package but this size has caused some other disadvantages.

Here you will find the common issues with the Amazon Echo Dot and how you can fix them.

- 1. Dot Responsiveness
  This complaint concerns the case when you have
  noticed that your Amazon Echo Dot has got the lack of

responsiveness or the proximity to your Dot so it could pick up your voice.

You can fix this issue if you re-run your voice training. If you haven't done it before then this is the reason why the Dot is not picking up your speech pattern or voice. Following these steps below, you can run your voice training:

1. Enter the Alexa app from your smart device.
2. Select **Settings** > **Voice Training** in the Alexa app
3. Check that you have selected the proper device from the top dropdown. This device will run the voice training.
4. Then select **Next** and you will be prompted to read aloud 25 phrases. While pronouncing these phrases, speak in your normal tone and also stand or sit your typical distance when you use your Echo Dot. If you have made your voice training right it will not awaken when you are across the room.

- Sound Quality

  The speaker is another disadvantage for some Dot users. Amazon Echo users don't know this problem because it has powerful speaker. But you can't expect the same from Echo Dot as it has smaller size. If you need a bigger sound you should have Amazon Echo.

  As for Dot's volume level, its full volume equals the half of the volume of Amazon Echo. Dot also doesn't have the same richness of sound like Amazon Echo. That's why Echo Dot may be not a good choice for a music speaker.

  You should connect your external speaker the 3.5mm jack to bypass the Echo Dot speakers completely. It should help to make the internal speakers disabled.

But at the same time, your external speakers must be turned on to enable communication with Alexa.

- Unexpected Device Limitations

You already know that the Alexa app can perform a lot of activities with the Echo Dot device. But to provide its proper work you must download the necessary skills within the Alexa application.

You can find all of the skills and features on the Alexa Help Page on Amazon.com. The functionality of Alexa is continuously growing. The developers are making more apps to function with Alexa every day.

If you need Alexa to perform specific tasks which are necessary for your everyday life you should know if Alexa can perform such tasks. In case if you purchase this device you could avoid unexpected limitations. You should make sure that Alexa is able to correspond your needs.

The advantage of working with IFTTT enables this device to connect to a variety of applications that Alexa may not be directly compatible with alone.

- Issues with the Alexa App

The developers of Alexa constantly update the Alexa app to make each of the Alexa devices more responsive and smarter. If you have got an message that says "The Alexa app is offline," you can fix it with a number of common solutions.

Here they are:

1. **Restarting your device**: When an Alexa error occurs you should restart your device. You should long press the sleep/wake button from your iPhone until the option appears on your screen to restart. You can do the same from an Android device, you should hold down your power button until the restart option appears on the screen.

2. **Force close the application**:

   In order to force close an application from your iPhone you should double press your Home button. Then you will see a slider of open applications on your screen. Then you should swipe the Alexa app upward to close it.

   Then navigate to the *Settings* on your device and select *Apps* or *Applications* from your Android device. You should find Alexa in the list of installed applications. You can clear data for your application if it is necessary. Amazon writes it is recommended to clear the data and select **Force Stop**.

3. **Uninstall the Application**: If you want to remove the application from your phone you should go to the Android device settings, select **Manage applications** and find Alexa in the listing of apps on your device. Then select **Uninstall.** You can also uninstall the application by long pressing on the Alexa app from your general applications section. When you have selected the app you should drag it to the top of the screen which should read **Uninstall** on the top left. Then press long the Alexa application from your iOS device until it begins to shake on your screen. When it starts shaking tap the 'X' on the app.

   After the uninstallation of the application you should navigate to your respective app store and re-download the application

- Dot is not responding to the wake word "Alexa."

  If you have completed the voice training but your Echo Dot is not responding when you say "Alexa" you should open the Alexa app and navigate to **Settings** and select **Wake Word.** In this app you are able to change the wake word to or from "Alexa".

- Dot cannot find my music or open the correct application.

  When you give some command to Alexa you must be always specific in what you need. Alexa can perform a lot of commands within the moment but if you have not spoken it properly the Echo Dot will not know how to perform your request.

  If you have such issues you should go through the Voice Training section which is described in this guide. It should help you to find commands that you did not know how to use. When you need Alexa to play music it requires specific instructions. Here are the examples:

- *"Play Sting on Spotify."* It is necessary to specify the name of application. Otherwise, Alexa may become confused and it will cause the command to fail. This command is able to shuffle music by this artist from Spotify.

- *"Play Spotify."* If Alexa gets this command it simply plays music where you last left off.

If you have purchased some music from the Digital Music Store or you have connected your personal music library you should give simple commands:

- *"Alexa, play Beyonce."*
- *"Alexa, play the new Shakira song."*
- *"Alexa, shuffle Michael Jackson."*

Here are other commands to control your music:

- *"Repeat this song,"*
- *"Next song"*
- *"Buy this song"*

Chapter 8: Troubleshooting Issues with Amazon Dot

This chapter should help you to find some quick answers to common issues if you are having some trouble with the Dot. In case if don't know what to do with troubleshooting, make sure you follow the right steps to fix any issues.

Your Amazon Echo Dot Ring

The ring of the Amazon Echo Dot is an indicator if something is wrong with the device. It may have six different color depending on the action.

Here is the description of each color:

Solid Blue and Cyan: You can see these colors after the wake word is spoken, during performing of the user's command and during Alexa's response to your command. While the initial boot process of your Echo Dot is going on you can see these colors.

Solid Red: A red light on your Echo Dot will appear if you select the mute button on the top of your Dot. And this light means your Dot is on Mute.

Orange Spinning Clockwise: If you see this color it means that Echo Dot is trying to connect to the wireless network.

White: If you are adjusting the volume on your device this color usually appears.

Wavering Violet: If your Echo Dot's ring has wavering violet color that means some error has happened during the setup of your wireless network.

If you have failed in connecting to your Wi-Fi, follow the next steps:

- Try to connect to your network again.
- Make sure you have entered the correct password for your network.
- Check the functionality of your Wi-Fi on other devices. If they cannot connect to it then the problem may be about connection.
- Try to update the firmware for your network device.
- Try to connect again away from any device that may interfere with the connection.
- You can reset your router with the help of the pinhole on its back. First, wait for the device to power up

completely. While waiting, reset your Echo Dot by unplugging the power adapter for a few seconds.

Issues with Sound

If your Echo Dot is having some issues with sound quality then you can try the following things to solve this issue. One of the reasons is may be an accent. Alexa is able to understand and get acclimated to your voice.   The Echo Dot of Second Generation is running better with this issue as it has an updated language processer and it identifies the user commands better.

If while giving some command to Alexa you see that Alexa is misconstruing your words you should attempt to run the voice training program again. You should make sure you are re-running your training in the normal conditions, the same like you would be using your device. You must not place your voice right next to the microphone when performing the training as you will never speak this way subsequently. You should perform your training at the same distance like you generally speak with Alexa.

If you turn of any background noise it may also help the Dot to pick up your voice specifically. You should know if you have done the voice training correctly on one Alexa device, all other devices will work better as well.

Once you have started your voice training the ring around your Amazon Echo will illuminate and you will need to read through 25 sentences. If you have said something wrong or not clear you can repeat your sentence before clicking **Next**.

After completing the voice training you have the option to complete the training again to further tune your results.

Issues with Alexa Discovering Your Smart Home Device

If while discovering your Smart Home device you are having some issues with your Echo Dot in this chapter you will get to know how to troubleshoot the connection.

One of the first things that you should do is to make sure that your new home device is compatible with your Echo Dot. You can find a supported list of devices at https://www.amazon.com/alexasmarthome. If your device is included on the list of supported items then you should double check to determine if a "skill" is needed to enable it to work with Alexa. There are two brands which do not need "skills" to be able to work with the Echo Dot. They are WeMo and Phillips.

Here are the instructions you should follow to properly troubleshoot your device.

- First, you should download the companion application for your smart home device and pass the standalone setup.

- Then make sure that your device is currently connected to the same Wi-Fi network as your Amazon Echo Dot.

- If you still have the same issue with your connection you should try restarting both devices.

- Then you should confirm that any software updates which are necessary for the home device have been performed.

- Then try to disable the skill associated with your home device and re-enable.

- You can also try discovering your devices again. You should just say to Alexa "Discover my devices" to place the Amazon Echo Dot in discoverable mode.

Echo Dot is Not Responding or Does Not Turn On

If your Echo Dot is not responding or not turning on you can try a lot of ways to make your device responsive again. You should follow the next steps:

- One of the easiest ways to troubleshoot this issue is to make sure that you are using the power adapter that comes with your devices. If you use the cellular device chargers or other low level power adapters you should know that they do not provide the needed power for the Echo Dot to operate properly.
- You should use the action button to see if Alexa will respond. After pushing the button, attempt to speak your command to Alexa again.
- When you are speaking to Alexa you should speak is clear and natural. Also, there must be no background noise.

- You should also make sure that your external speaker is at least 3 feet away from the Echo Dot and it does not interfere with sound quality. It must be at least 8 inches from a wall or various other objects.

In most cases when the Echo Dot refuses to listen to voice commands you can solve this by unplugging then re-plugging the device back in again. Sometimes it happens due to a software update, or because the Internet connection was interrupted. Normally the Echo Dot operates by sending a question or phrase spoken to it to Amazon's servers, which interpret the command and tell it how to respond. In some cases restarting the Echo may not help it. Alternatively, you can try to leave it unplugged for a few hours and then plug it back in. Some users have reported that it solved the issue. It may also happen because of another unrelated issue, like software updates or issues communicating with the Amazon servers. If Echo Dot still does not work properly or at all, you should refer to the previous section that describes how to perform a factory reset. You will have to be set up again on an Amazon account and Wi-Fi network if you reset. In most cases it may fix the problem. If nothing else is working you should contact Amazon's customer support through their website. The customer service team can assist with a repair or replacement if you have already tried resetting and restarting Dot.

Bluetooth Connectivity Issues with Your Echo Dot

If your Echo Dot is having some issues while connecting to Bluetooth you should follow these steps to overcome it:

Interference: If Bluetooth is not functioning as it is supposed you should try moving your device away from anything that could potentially influence the connection. The possible interferences may be baby monitors, microwaves, or other wireless devices.

- **Battery Life**: One of the reasons of bad Bluetooth connection is the battery life of your device. If you cannot remove your battery, make sure that it is full charged. If the batteries of your device are removable and/or rechargeable you should replace or recharge the batteries.

- **Clear All Bluetooth Devices:** The other way to rectify connectivity issues is to clear and reconnect the Bluetooth device. You should navigate to *Settings* from the left navigation panel to clear your Bluetooth device. Then you should select your Alexa Device in the Settings and select *Bluetooth* > *Clear*.

  Pair a New Bluetooth Device: You can also clear all devices and reconnect a new one which is the best way to test a Bluetooth device. You should select your Alexa device and then select *Bluetooth* > *Pair a New Device*. When your device enters pairing mode you should select the device from your cellular device. You will know if your device is connected successfully when Alexa notifies you.

Streaming Issues with the Echo Dot

Normally your Wi-Fi connection may determine the streaming issues with your Dot. You can fix these issues following the next steps:

- **Reduce Wi-Fi Congestion**: You should reduce Wi-Fi congestion simply by turning off devices that you do not use to free bandwidth on your network. If your device is placed close to the ground or on the floor you should raise the device higher and move it away from any walls as they may be blocking the signal. If it does not solve the problem you should move your device closer to the router/modem.

- **Reset Your Device**: You should also restart your Echo Dot as well as the modem to fix streaming issues. You can simply press and hold down the Microphone and Volume Down buttons at the same time. You should hold it until the light ring on your device turns orange. When the process is completed the light ring should turn blue then turn on and off again. Then navigate to your Alexa application and set up your Wi-Fi again.

- **Restart Your Device**: You can also restart your Amazon Echo by unplugging the power adapter from the wall or from the back of the device. Then you should wait a few seconds and plug your device back in.

- **Restart Your Network Device**: If you are still having issues with network connectivity of your device you should try resetting your router or modem. It is easy to do by unplugging the network device or pressing the pin hole on the back of the network device. When you have completely rebooted your device you should give your Echo Dot time to connect and retry your original action.

- **Contact Your Internet Service Provider**: If all the recommendations do not help to solve the issue you should contact your Internet Service Provider for more help troubleshooting your network connection.

Bluetooth Connectivity Issues with Your Echo Dot and the Alexa Voice Remote

Simple to Set Up & Use

1. Plug in Echo Dot
2. Connect to the internet with the Alexa App
3. Just ask for music, weather, news, and more

If you have connected your Echo Dot with your Alexa Voice Remote but it does not work properly, you can fix it with the help of the following solutions.

- **New Batteries**: First, check the batteries as they may have lost charge. If it is so, then insert the new AAA batteries in the correct orientations into your Alexa Voice Remote.

- **Pair Remote Again**: If you have noticed that your device is not working properly with your Dot you should go into Alexa Dot settings and select the device which your remote is paired and then select ***Forget Remote***.

  When you have done this you should run through the device setup again with Echo Dot and the Alexa Voice Remote.

- **Restart Your Echo Dot:** If none of the options have helped you to fix this issue you should restart your device. You should simply unplug the power adapter from your device and then plug it back in.

Chapter 9: Amazon Echo Dot and Others

The invention of such devices like the Amazon Echo, Amazon Tap, and the Amazon Echo Dot has enable Amazon to monopolize the home-based hub industry. But at the same time some competitors have appeared. The major competitors of Amazon are the Google Home and Apple's innovations with Siri.

You can find other alternatives which are not so popular like Google and Apple offers. But no one can beat the Amazon Echo in terms of price point.

Echo Dot (Generation 1) vs. Echo Dot (Generation 2)

The Echo Dot Second Generation has been designed with the enhanced features. The most noticeable change in the new Echo Dot is its smaller size and its use of volume buttons than the volume ring. The Amazon Dot First Generation contained a LED power light that the current Echo Dot does not have. The second generation Echo Dot does not include the 3.5mm cable that the first generation Echo Dot has in its packaging. You can also purchase the second generation Dot in white pearl color which the first Dot does not have.

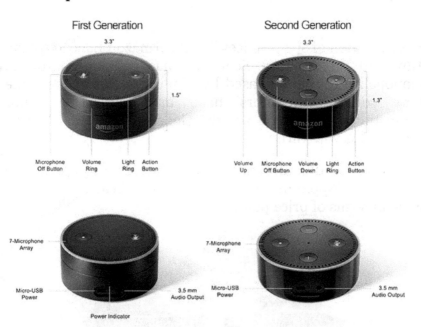

The Echo Dot 1 and 2 have the same specifications but its internal workings have some changes. The Dot 2 has got the same seven far-field microphones as the first design and a new speech processer was incorporated to improve the speech accuracy on the new generation.

The Echo Dot Second Generation also has Echo Spatial Perception or ESP. It is helpful if you have multiple Alexa devices to enable one device to respond. This feature was not included in the first generation suite of Alexa devices but they will soon update this software and it will have ESP.

The Echo Dot First generation was being criticized a lot for its limited quantities. Amazon has improved this device in many ways. It has become more available to its consumers via the Amazon website as well as Best Buy. Amazon has also decreased the price by nearly half the amount of the first which cost $89.99. Now you can buy the Echo Dot for $49.99. Except these significant changes they have also slashed the length of the warranty, having decreased the warranty from 1 year to only 90 days.

Echo Dot vs. Google Home

The newest competitor of Alexa products is the Google Home. The price policy is different as the Google Home cost $130 comparing with the Dot priced at $49. The Home also has a "wake word" that is "*Okay Google.*" The Google tries its best to win for customers but its design is not sophisticated like the Dot's which is available in two colors and it has different fabric cases to change. Besides, Google has not mentioned about the integration of Home with smart home products. Unlike the Google Home the Alexa products have more developed features and they are more popular in technologic market.

Echo Dot vs. Apple

Apple is considered to be an unofficial competitor of Amazon. This company is always trying to win various technology-focused markets. For this moment, Apple has not officially announced the release of a home-based system but they try their best to make some changes about Siri.

The SDK for Siri has been recently opened. It's an important event for the developers as now they can build Siri's voice command functionality to their applications. Uber is also trying to gear up for the change. They have announced that soon the users will be able to use voice commands to book rides with Uber. Apple also has released a home application in conjunction with Apple's Homekit platform. Different HomeKit smart home appliances may be controlled by this application.

The Echo Dot stays quite ahead of Apple in this area as it doesn't need direct interaction with a user's cellular device. Besides, the Echo Dot has much more other specifications to stay top device in the technology market.

Chapter 10: Echo Dot VS Amazon Echo and Amazon Tap

<u>A Quick Overview of Amazon Echo:</u>

The Amazon Echo is a wireless smart speaker. This twenty-first-century device is able to become your personal assistant. You will feel like you've got your own digital assistant that can make your life easier as it has a wide range of functionality.

Apart from devices like Siri and Cortana, Amazon Echo is able to recognize and process different voice commands through the Alexa OS and outside your smartphone device. Alexa can hear you from anywhere as it has omnidirectional speakers and microphones. It can be activated in any place of your home. After training on voice recognition, Alexa will understand different users even with their specific dialect or accent.

Amazon Echo Dot:

This is the mini version of the Echo cylinder. It comes with a basic speaker so it can function in a smaller and lighter format. One of the advantages is that Dot is able to connect with a user's own wired or wireless speakers, while the full-sized Echo can't do it for this moment. Dot has got the same Alexa-based voice-recognition system and it can connect Bluetooth or 3.5mm plug speakers. Dot can perform the same functions like the full size Amazon Echo.

One of the functions of Dot is that it is able to place orders on Amazon. It also can get current news and weather, stream music, live media and also full integration with smart home products. You can use your Dot anywhere in your house, in as many rooms as you want. You can set one in the kitchen to control your smart appliances, then use the other in the gym for playing music during your workout and ask whatever you want while resting in the living-room or set one for a wake up alarm in your bed-room.

As the integration with the Dot and Echo products continues soon Amazon Prime customers who already have an Echo device or Alexa-enabled Amazon Fire TV will have more advantages. For this moment, the Echo Dot is only available through Alexa Voice shopping.

Which one is better is for you to decide. You can use the Amazon Echo in one room of the house to give simple or complex tasks. Echo Dot can offer the same functionality but in a smaller format. Echo Dot is a portable version of the Echo and you can easily move it from room to room or keep it in every room of the house. The speaker of Amazon Dot is basic so it will sound like in streaming music.

Amazon Tap:

The Amazon Tap is also a small wireless and Bluetooth enabled, but not voice-activated. The Tap has up to 9 hours of battery life. This version doesn't have a "Wake word" unlike the Echo and the Echo Dot, that's why it is not always listening. If you want to activate it you must tap a button, hence it is named "Tap".

The main difference between the Amazon Tap and the Echo Dot is that the Dot must be "wired", plugged in in the socket and activated by the "Wake word". Besides, the speaker in the Echo Dot is smaller and less powerful than the Amazon Echo and the Tap.

The Amazon Tap may be less convenient than the Echo and Echo Dot not only because of tapping the activation button but also it must be connected to Wi-Fi for Alexa to work. This way you must connect your Amazon Tap to a public Wi-Fi or use your Smartphone or other portable internet device, some kind of a hot-spot.

Another feature is that Alexa Voice Remote is compatible with the Amazon Echo and Echo Dot but it not compatible with the Amazon Tap.

Conclusion

The Amazon Echo Dot Second Generation is not only a sleek design, a small package, and a big brain. It's full of new options and advantages comparing with the previous version Amazon Echo First Generation. It has absolutely new size, versatility and intelligence.

The Echo Dot is only one in a line of many devices which is able to speak to Alexa. This way Amazon Dot is a perfect home control device. As Alexa keeps all necessary information at your fingertips, it is able to control your home devices. In fact, Amazon Dot in some way better than Amazon Echo. For example, Alexa, on the Fire TV, can't control non-cloud based smart home devices. But Dot can control the same smart home devices and use all the same services.

You can get more benefits with Amazon Echo Second generation. You can get to know the state of traffic, order Domino's pizza, ask for weather and much more.

Alexa on your Echo Dot can become your life manager. This is the assistant that conform to your wishes and requests. It's able to learn and improve its skills. It will make your life organized, prepared, on time, and entertained. Whatever command you give it will update its skills. There are no similar competitors which are able to suggest the same variety of skills and benefits that the Amazon Alexa-enabled devices can.

This incredible device is able change your life. It will become easier and smarter. Whether you have one, two or even six devices, the Echo Dot will serve you perfectly to meet your requirements for the most innovative device.

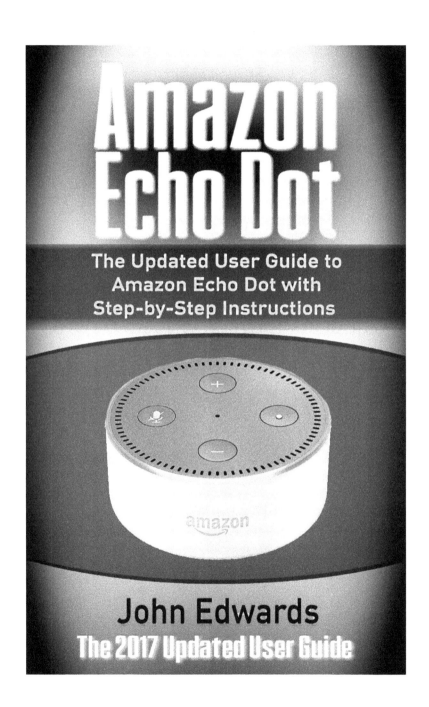

Amazon Echo Dot

The Updated User Guide to Amazon Echo Dot with Step-by-Step Instructions

John Edwards

The 2017 Updated User Guide

Amazon Echo Dot
The Updated User Guide to Amazon Echo Dot with Step-by-Step Instructions (Amazon Echo, Amazon Echo Guide, user manual, by amazon, smart devices)

JOHN EDWARDS

CONTENTS

Introduction

In this book you will read about the latest updates of Amazon Echo Dot. If you know the basic information about setting, location, home control and the Amazon Echo Dot features this book will be interesting for you as it gives the most necessary information what is new in Amazon Echo Dot features and capabilities.
If you know only the basics of Amazon Echo Dot now it's time to know more features that Amazon Echo Dot can do. Controlling your home is not the only popular features within the Amazon Echo Dot. It is able to do much more than you think.

In this guide you will learn about:
- Grouping Your Smart Home Devices
- Getting Flight Information
- Reading Kindle books
- Connecting with Wikipedia
- Getting Flight Information
- Listening to various radio stations
- And much more

The greatest feature of Amazon Echo Dot is that you can customize it to your daily routine and lifestyle. It is an amazing smart device that gives you a lot of possibilities to make your life more convenient, smart, fun and easy.

Having Alexa at its core, the Amazon Echo Dot is getting better and better. This Alexa enabled device can be customized with the skills that respond your lifestyle most of all. Your Echo Dot will enable you to be productive and get things done. You can check schedules, update events, order supplies and much more with Amazon Echo Dot.

The Amazon Echo Dot is simple and sleek. It is a truly innovative device that is able to make your world fun and smart.

Chapter 1: What is the Amazon Echo Dot?

The Amazon Echo Dot is a small powerhouse in the form of the hockey puck that has lots of features. It is a small Bluetooth speaker that is equipped with the same options and features that the first generation Amazon Dot had and even more.

Here are the main characteristics:

- Designated Microphone Button (off/on)
- Far field voice capabilities (long range)
- Wi-Fi Action Button
- Amazon Alexa
- Wide array of skills

Features & Characteristics of the Amazon Echo Dot

The Amazon Echo Dot has a wide range of features that you can customize to your needs. It suits any lifestyle, age and profession. It may be useful for a child, student, businessman, old man... It can perform so many tasks from ordering pizza to getting flight and traffic information. It depends on your lifestyle preference.

It also gives you the option to alternate between Bluetooth connectivity and use of the 3.5mm audio port. The integration of Echo Spatial Perception enables the multiple device users to interact with the device closest to them. It provides in case if you have 7 Echo Dot devices that all seven not to run your commands.

Here is the list of the most prominent features within the Echo Dot with the explanations how they interact with you and the device.

1. **Using an External Speaker w/ the Echo Dot:** As the Amazon Echo Dot is a bluetooth speaker, it is not able to be connected with an external speaker. The external speaker is able to do what the small speaker can't and to enable the music to play from the Dot with a fuller sound.

2. **Use of the Amazon Voice Remote:** The new Echo Dot may be connected with the Voice Remote via Bluetooth. It may be used as an alternative to some voice commands.

3. **Alexa Skills:** The Amazon Echo Dot, like all Alexa enabled devices, is able to utilize the wide variety of skills that Alexa can perform. The skills present the functionalities paired with such stores as Amazon,

Uber, Dominoes or even StubHub. The user can add these functionalities to his Echo Dot via Alexa App.

4. Media & Your Echo Dot:

You can listen not only to music with your Echo Dot but also various forms of media such as books, podcasts, radio programs and much more. In most cases you will need a premium subscription. In other cases you can connect your personal music library using Alexa if you do not hold subscription. Here is the list of subscription services compatible with Alexa:

- Amazon Music Unlimited
- Amazon Music
- Spotify Premium
- Prime Music
- iHeartRadio
- Audible
- TuneIn

You can also use Audible and Kindle with you Echo Dot if you need to stream audiobooks, newspaper and magazine subscriptions. You can use the following commands in order to play music from the default music application:

"Play Chris Brown on Pandora" – (This command chooses the station you designate) If you do not mention the application name the command will run only if the default music player is set. In other case, it will look for Amazon Prime.

- *"Play Pandora"* – If you tell this command the music will play where you last left off within the application.

If your personal music library is connected to Amazon or you have purchased music from the Amazon Prime, you can give not so specific commands if Amazon is chosen as default music player. In other cases, the music would play in your default application. Here is the list of commands:

- *"Alexa, play Mariah Carey."*
- *"Alexa, shuffle Maroon 5. "*
- *"Alexa, play the new Taylor Swift song."*

5. ***News, Weather & Traffic Information:***

You can also use your Echo Dot and other Alexa devices to get updates on up-to-date news headlines , weather updates, sports data and movie theater ShowTime information. Besides, you can get regular traffic updates and you will never be late for work with the help of Alexa.

6. *General Information:*

You can ask Alexa some simple questions concerning holidays, television or movie programs and information about popular and well-known people.

7. *Calendars & Alarms:*

You can also keep on schedule and on time using your Echo Dot. If you used to planning or relying on your calendar, your Echo Dot may be very helpful. You can add and review any calendar events with the Amazon Echo Dot through Alexa's linked calendar.

In case if you want to add events you should link the calendar within the Alexa mobile application. You can do this with the following commands.

Navigate to Settings> Calendar > and select Google Calendar. Then choose "Link Google Calendar Account" to link your active Google calendar.

Here is the list of commands for interacting with the calendar.
- "What's on my calendar on [day]?"

- "When is my next event?"
- "Add [event] to my calendar for [day] at [time]."

You can set alarms on the Echo Dot 24 hours in advance. Besides, you can also set timers using your Echo Dot. And you can alter both within the Alexa Mobile Application.

Once you have set the alarm via voice you can alter it within the application. You can also change the volume and alarm sound within the Alexa app.

You can use a number of alarm setting within Alexa application:
- "Wake me up at 6 AM"
- "What time is my alarm set for today?"
- "Set a repeating alarm from Monday to Friday at 5AM"

Timers have their own set of options. You should know that you can't change the timer's volume by changing the volume of the device.

Here is the list of commands you can use while working with timers:
- "Set the timer for 20 mins"
- "Set a timer for 5AM

You can also manage the lists except calendars and alarms, using the Echo Dot. They include shopping or to do lists. You can also link the third party list services.

8. **Integration with Voicecast:**

You can send content automatically to your fire tablet using Voicecast. Working with Alexa features, this service may include Music, Wikipedia, lists, weather and much more.

Here is the list of Alexa features that Voicecast works with:
- Music
- Wikipedia
- Flash Briefing
- Lists
- Weather
- Timer and alarms
- Questions and answers
- Help

9. **Shopping with the Echo Dot:**

Shopping with the Echo Dot is easy and pleasant. This is one of the most advertised services. You can buy music, order an Alexa Device and place orders with Alexa.

You can also add the items to your Amazon cart and access your purchase history or order eligible items through Alexa.

You can purchase eligible items with the Amazon Echo Dot if the order amount for each item is not more than 12. You should follow these instruction to do so:

- Order a [item name] – You may be asked to answer of yes or no to confirm the order once the Dot has found the product.
- "Reorder [item name]" – You may be asked to answer of yes or no to confirm the order once the Dot has found the product
- "Add [item name] to my cart" – The selected item will be added to your cart on Amazon.com.
- "Cancel my order" – You can only cancel an order immediately after you have completed/placed it.

The Echo Dot is also able to purchase music through Amazon. You can set up an optional confirmation code and use it before starting your music purchase. This is just to make sure that the purchases will not be made by mistake. It also helps to prevent anyone from buying music on your account.

Here are the guidelines when attempting to buy music using your Echo Dot:

- "Shop for the album Maroon 5 (Insert album name)"

- "Shop for the song Stay by Rihanna (Insert Track Name & Artist)"
- You can also tell the Echo Dot to buy the current song command when a song is currently playing on an Amazon supported station. You should just say, "Buy this song."

You can check your order status via the echo Dot. If you have some undelivered orders Alexa will give you information about the status of the order with a scheduled date closest to the current date.

10. **IFTT Integration:** Using IFTTT integration you can link items that were not found in the skills library with applications and websites. Owing to this service multiple devices and application may be connected with one another in the form of recipes.

Follow these instructions to connect your Dot to IFTTT:

5. First, navigate to the Alexa Channel page from the IFTTT application and select the 'Connect' button.
6. Then you should sign into your Amazon account. It must be the same account that you use with the Amazon Echo Dot. Then select "I Agree" to move forward on the 'additional information screen".

And your account will now be connected with Amazon.

7. Then you will have the option of turning on any predefined recipes and set them to fit your individual needs.

IFTT enables you to generate and use formulas to run with your smart home devices. Your Echo Dot and IFTTT are able to work with applications like Phillips Hue, SmartThings and Harmony.
Using IFTTT you can manipulate of light colors, turning lights on, locking doors and the toggling of device power.

You can also create new formulas or strings of actions using IFTT website. You can do it easily by logging into your account and selecting the 'Create New Recipe' link or search for the application you need.

1. Once you have selected the action or the application you should proceed to choose a trigger from the variety selected.
2. Then you should complete the field labeled, trigger.
3. Then choose the desired action path.
4. And choose an action associated with your product or initial choice.
5. Once you have completed all of the needed steps you will be able to use your trigger with the chosen product.

These are not all the things your Amazon Echo Dot is able to do. One of the popular features of the Echo Dot is its ability to work as a smart home hub.

You can place the Amazon Echo Dot in virtually any room for any purpose. The Amazon Dot is able to work with lots of devices that will make your home smarter and more convenient. You can buy any of the smart options with the Dot from Amazon.com or alone through Amazon.com.

You can use your Echo Dot in conjunction with a number of smart home devices. Here are the most used devices:
- o Phillips Hue Starter Kit
- o The Bose Soundlink Mini II
- o *TP-Link Smart Plug*
- o ecobee3 Smart Thermostat

Settings of the Amazon Echo Dot

The Settings within the Alexa comprise so much information that relates to your Amazon Echo Dot.

This information includes the following:
- The listing of your Alexa enabled devices
- The option to set up a new Alexa enabled devices
- Voice Training: You can adapt your Alexa enabled products by voice training specifically to your voice so if someone has an accent the devices will be able to understand you better.

- Account Information: It includes account information for Music & Media, Flash Briefings, sports updates, calendar, lists and traffic.

o Music & Media: It includes the account information for Amazon Music, Spotify, Pandora, iHeartRadio and TuneIn.

o Flash Briefing: Flash Briefing information is given from NPR Hourly, NPR TuneIn and weather from Amazon. You can also get flash briefing information from TechCrunch, Slate, Harvard Business and many more.

o Sports Update: You can hear score and scheduling updates from various teams as they are added to this section. You should search for the name of the team you would like or select the 'x' if you want to delete a team from the list.

o Traffic: You can set the 'From address' to receive any directions beginning from this location in this section. You can add various stops and the 'To' location so to have an end point for your traffic updates.

o Calendars: It includes all the calendars that you would like to link with your device. If you want a new calendar you can choose it from the drop down menu which comprises all of the linked Gmail calendars.

o Lists: You can manage Alexa lists in two lists including Todoist and Anydo.

- Voice Purchasing: You can turn on the option to make purchases by voice in this section. You can also set up a four digit pin to confirm purchases and update your 1 click payment settings within this area.

- Household Profile: If you join a household you will be able to share material with other household members. You can also share across Alexa devices.

Chapter 2: Comparing the Echo Dot 1st Generation, Echo Dot 2nd Generation and the Amazon Echo

Despite the fact that the Amazon Echo 1st and 2nd generation have the same features but there is something that the Amazon Echo Dot 2nd Generation can do better than the previous version.

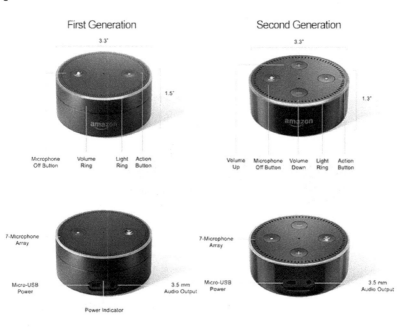

Let's see what it is. The difference is not only about the size but also about the features. Let's start comparing with the external characteristics. First of all, the Echo Dot has slightly smaller size. And if you place the two items next to each other you will see that the Amazon Echo Dot 2nd generation is shorter and it utilizes a simpler design. The rotation dial for volume has also been replaced with volume buttons in the Amazon Echo 2nd Generation comparing with its predecessor. You can also control the volume with your voice that it easier. The next difference is about the LED power light which the Echo Dot 2nd generation does not have. The new version has a new glossy finish. Besides, the Amazon Echo Dot has got enhanced features.

Comparing the internal characteristics of the Amazon Dot 1st and the Amazon Echo Dot 2nd generation there are some differences. The Amazon Echo Dot 2nd Generation has a new speech processor to enhance its speech accuracy. The Echo Dot 2nd Generation also has Echo Spatial Perception (ESP). This feature is helpful when you use the Echo Dot in conjunction with multiple in home devices to provide only one Dot to respond. The Echo Dot 1st generation is able to gain the access to this feature via a software update.

You can notice the differences in the box that comes with the Echo Dot 2nd Generation. The new version of the Echo Dot does not have the 3.5mm cable like the original predecessor. The Echo Dot 2nd Generation is also available in white color unlike the Echo Dot 1st generation.

For this moment, the 2nd Generation is more accessible to purchase than the first version. You can purchase it not only on Amazon's website but also at Best Buy stores as well. Originally you could order the Echo Dot 1st generation via an Alexa device. But the Amazon Echo Dot 2nd generation cost the half price comparing with the Amazon Echo 1st generation. The first version of the Echo Dot cost $89.99. And now you can buy the Amazon Echo Dot 2nd generation for $49.99. Buying a new Echo Dot, you get a new warranty available to users. It is only 90 days unlike 1-year warranty that the Amazon Echo Dot 1st generation has.

Advantages & Disadvantages of the Echo Dot 1 & 2 Generation

Any product has both advantages and disadvantages. The Amazon Echo Dot is not an exception. Despite it is an upgraded version, it is not flawless.

Here are some disadvantages that it includes:

a. The responsiveness of the Echo Dot is important for the usability of the device. You can update it using the voice training within the Alexa mobile Application. Making the voice training is a good way to keep good interaction and voice connection with your Amazon Echo Dot. If you have not done the voice training yet then your Echo Dot might not work properly. You can run the voice training by following the next steps:

5. First, open the Alexa Application from your mobile device.
6. Then select the Menu button in the top left corner and choose 'Settings' > 'Voice Training'
7. You should select the device in which you would like to run the voice training on.
8. Then select 'Next'. You will be prompted to read the next 25 statements aloud. It is important to speak in your normal tone and not to get too close or be too far away from the Echo Dot.

b. The Echo Dot is not designed to be used solely for its speaker. The Echo Dot also has Bluetooth capability and it may be connected with an external speaker.

c. Echo Dot may not find the correct application
d. Troubleshooting issues w/ the Alexa Mobile Application
e. If your Echo Dot does not respond to the wake word when you speak it, then it is necessary to run the voice training again. If you have done your voice training before then you should make sure that your wake word is actually what you think it is. You should go into the Alexa app and ensure that the 'wake word' is Alexa or whatever you are saying. It

may be accomplished by going to your 'Settings' and selecting "Wake Word". In this section you can change and verify your wake word.

Even having all these disadvantages, they may be overcome and rectified.

Comparing the Amazon Echo Dot and the Amazon Echo

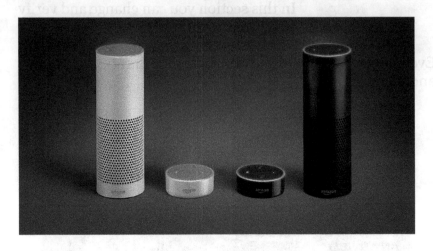

Amazon Echo Dot Specifications

Release Date: 2015 (United States) 2016 (United Kingdom)
Price: $179
Dimensions: 235mm x 83.5mm x 83.5
Weight: 1045 grams or 2.3 pounds
Connectivity: Bluetooth, dual band, dual-antenna, Wi-Fi (MIMO)
Power: Plugs into a wall outlet
Audio: 360 Degree Speaker – 2.5-inch woofer/2.5-inch tweeter
Alexa: Alexa is always enabled and always listening

Echo Dot
Specifications

Release Date: September of 2016
Price: $49
Dimensions: 38mm x 84mm x 84mm
Weight: 250 grams or .55 pounds
Connectivity: Bluetooth, dual-antenna, Wi-Fi (MIMO)

Power: Plugs into a wall outlet
Audio: 360 Degree Speaker for voice feedback only, Ability to connect to external speaker
Alexa: Alexa is always enabled and always listening

Despite its small size comparing with the Amazon Echo, the Amazon Echo Dot is able to perform the same Alexa skills and functions as the Echo.

Equipped with a sensational seven far-field microphone array, that the Amazon Echo also has, the Amazon Echo Dot guarantees you the same voice recognition within the Echo Dot like the Echo has.

One of the major differences is the sound quality of the Amazon Echo. Unlike its predecessor, the Echo Dot does not provide as strong sound as the Echo does. But you can solve it by connecting another speaker. The Amazon Echo Dot also has the ability to connect to external speakers whereas the Echo uses its own speaker.

The speaker within the Echo Dot may not be the most powerful but for everyday interactions with the Dot this quality is fine.

The following chart represents the contrast and similarities between the Amazon Echo and the Amazon Echo Dot 2nd Generation.

	Amazon Echo	Echo Dot (Gen. 2)
Amazon Alexa	Yes	Yes
Skills	Yes	Yes
Integration with IFTTT	Yes	Yes
Wake Word Activation	Yes	Yes
Connection w/ External Bluetooth Speaker	No	Yes
3.5mm Audio Jack	No	Yes
USB Cabling & Standard Power Adapter	Yes	Yes
Far Field Voice Capability	Yes	Upgraded
Echo Spatial Perception (ESP)	No	Yes
Wi-Fi Action Button	Yes	Yes
Choice of Color	Black or White	Black or White
Price	$180	$50

Chapter 3: Device Layout of the Amazon Echo Dot 2nd Generation

The Amazon Echo Dot's layout is simple enough for understanding how it works. It shows maximum functionality and it does not have too many buttons.

| Volume Up | Microphone Off Button | Volume Down | Light Ring | Action Button |

Having only 4 buttons, you can easily handle main functions of your Echo Dot. Here is the picture of the Amazon Echo Dot taken from Amazon.com to show its layout.

The Amazon Echo Dot includes:

- Volume Up button to maximize the volume as needed
- Volume Down button to minimizes the volume as needed
- Microphone Off Button to turn off the microphone so no commands can be given. If you enable it the device will not 'wake' when you use the 'wake' word.
- Action Button is able to turn off an alarm or a timer. It is also able to wake up the device.
- Light Ring is able to change colors depending on the actions that the Echo Dot is taking. The light ring usually shows if something is wrong or if an action is taking place. It has 6 different colors that may illuminate around the ring of the Echo Dot.

Solid Blue & Cyan – These colors start illuminating after the wake word is said, when a command is being given showing Alexa's response.   You can also see them when the Echo Dot is being booted.

Solid Red – This light shows that the Echo Dot has been set on mute. You can do it by selecting the microphone button on top of the Echo Dot.

Orange Spinning Clockwise – The orange light shows that the Echo Dot is connecting to the wireless network.
White – It shows that you are adjusting the volume on the device.

Wavering Violet – This color indicates that an error has occurred while attempting to connect to the wireless network.

 The Amazon Echo Dot has a micro-USB slot for powering the Echo Dot, the 7 far field microphone array and the 3.5mm Audio Output slot. You can see it on the image above taken from Amazon.com.

The Amazon Echo Dot weighs 163 grams and it is sized at 1.3" x 3.3" x 3.3". It supports Wi-Fi connectivity of dual band 802.11 a/b/g/n networks.

It is also able to support streaming of audio from your mobile phone to the Echo Dot. You can also connect the Echo Dot to an external speaker and the Echo Dot supports Bluetooth. However, while connecting, any Bluetooth device may require a PIN.

Chapter 4: The Amazon Echo Dot's Capabilities

How to Get Flight and Transportation Information with your Echo Dot

If you are planning your trip the Echo Dot is also able to help you with it. For example, you can obtain flight information. You don't need to pick up your mobile device as Alexa is able to look for the flights. You just need to use your voice and tell the information about the flight that would suit you best, depending on the upcoming trip information and the options for pricing.

You can set your home airport within Alexa to make sure that your flight information is accurate and personal.

Here are the skills that work in conjunction with Alexa to help you in travel and to provide you with flight information:

1. **Landing Times:** You can get landing times free once you have enabled it. And you can get flight information based on flight numbers. Here is the list of airlines that it supports: Virgin America, Spirit, United, Frontier, Alaska, Delta, Air Canada, American, Southwest, Hawaiian and Porter.

You can simply say: *"Alexa, ask Landing Times when Southwest flight ...(number of flight) lands"*

Skyscanner: If you enable Skyscanner you can get estimated pricing before beginning the actual booking process as this flight search skill is free to enable. It usually shows the most recent lowest prices found.

You can say: *"Alexa, ask Skyscanner to find me a flight to Los Angeles tomorrow"*

2. **Kayak**: You can get the real time flight information with the use of Kayak's flight tracker. You can also check the prices of rental cars and hotels along with flight information
   You can ask: *"Alexa, where can I go for $400?"*

3. **Flight Guru**: Flight Guru gives flight information based on flight number. When you use the flight number you can get the flight status and landing information.

Setting Up Your Alexa to Receive Flight Information w/ Kayak

1. First, open the Alexa mobile application from your mobile device or tablet.
2. Then select Skills from the left menu.
3. Search for 'Kayak' and select the newly found skill.
4. Then select 'Enable Skill' from the Skill's home screen.
5. After enabling this skill in the application you can use with your Alexa enabled Echo Dot.
6. Once you have enabled this skill you will be able to search and get pricing using the regular Alexa voice commands.

Here is the list of commands for this skill in statements or questions:

- "Alexa, ask Kayak where I can go for $250"
- "Alexa, ask Kayak when the Flight from New York will land in London"
- "Alexa, ask Kayak how much it cost to fly from Los Angeles to Toronto"

Setting Up Your Alexa to Receive Flight Information w/ Sky Scanner

1. First, open the Alexa mobile application from your mobile device or tablet.
2. Then select Skills from the left menu.
3. Find 'SkyScanner' and select the newly found skill.
4. Then you should select 'Enable Skill' from the Skill's home screen.
5. Once you have enabled the skill in the application you can use it with your Alexa enabled Echo Dot.
6. After enabling this skill, you can search and get pricing using the regular Alexa voice commands.

Here are the commands for this skill may include statements or questions:

- "Alexa, ask Sky Scanner to find me a flight for Friday to New York"
- "Alexa, ask SkyScanner where I can go this Monday"
- "Alexa, open SkyScanner"

You should know that these skills will not take you through the booking process as they are only for informational purposes.

How to Use Your Amazon Echo Dot to Read with Kindle

If you are a keen reader the Echo Dot may become a good companion to add some books to any library or study. You can use Echo Dot to read an eligible selection of books with its text-to-speech technology, many other news articles and Wikipedia articles.

Here is the list of eligible selections that you can read using the Amazon Echo Dot:
- Items from the Kindle Owners' Lending Library
- Items shared I your Family Library
- Items borrowed through Kindle Unlimited
- Items purchased from the Kindle Store

You can also find eligible Alexa Books in the Alexa mobile application. You can do it by selecting Music & Books > Kindle Books > Books Alexa can read.

For this moment, reading of comic books, speed of narration control and immersion reading are not supported by Alexa.

When you tell Alexa to read books you should know that Alexa will not start the book over again. She will read from the point at which you left off in any Amazon Devices.

You can also move to different chapter in the book by utilizing the Now Playing bar that may be done within Alexa application. And you can also choose a chapter from the queue list.

Here is the number of commands that you can tell Alexa to interact with Kindle through the Amazon Echo Dot:

- "Read my book, [insert book title here]"
- "Play the Kindle book, [insert book title]"
- "Read [insert book title]"
- "Go back" – if you want to go to a previous paragraph
- "Go forward" – it means to go to the next paragraph
- "Play"
- "Skip back" – it means to go to a previous paragraph
- "Skip ahead" – it means to go to the next paragraph
- "Stop"
- "Pause"
- "Next" – it means to go to the next paragraph
- "Previous" – it means to go to a previous paragraph

Setting up You Amazon Echo Dot with Kindle

1. You should open the Kindle Application from your mobile device in order to start this process.
2. Then you should select **Music & Books** from the left navigation menu.
3. Then select Kindle Books from the bottom of the menu.

4. You can see only the supported Kindle Books under the heading, Books Alexa Can Read.
5. Then you should Select one of the supported books from the list and Alexa will start to read on the Echo Dot.

How to Use Your Echo Dot for References

If you need to know the definition of any word or you are not sure about spelling of some word the Amazon Echo Dot is able to help you with it. It can perform a great variety of skills that may help you with spelling words, getting facts, defining words and many other skills.

Even without enabling any of these skills the Echo Dot can give you answers to dictionary and spelling related questions.

Here is the list of command that may help you to search information you need:

"Alexa, spell the word "miscellaneous"

"Alexa, what is the definition of the word "miscellaneous"?"

And here are the skills that provide this functionality:

1. **Word of the Day:** You can enable this skill free and get a word everyday with definitions and examples from the website wordnik.com. If you want to use this skill with Alexa , just say:

   a. "Alexa, ask Word of the Day for today's word"

   b. "Alexa, open Word of the Day"

2. **Quick Word Spell**: Once you have enabled this skill free you can get the spelling of words on the fly and as needed. You should just say the following commands to use this skill:

   a. "Alexa, ask Quick Word to spell "squirrel"

   b. "Alexa, ask Quick Word to spell "crocodile"

3. **Word Source**: You can get to know about the origin of words with this skill. If you need to use this skill you should simply say:

   a. "Alexa, ask Word Source about the word basket"

   b. "Alexa, ask Word Source what is the origin of the "chassis"

How to Group Your Smart Home Devices

One of the advantages of the Amazon Echo Dot is that you can use it with your smart home devices. After grouping your devices together you can easily control multiple devices and multiple rooms at once.

You can to create a group of smart home devices within the Alexa application to be able to control multiple smart home devices all at once.

How to create a Smart Home Group on Your Echo Dot

5. You should open the Alexa mobile application from your mobile device and locate Smart Home from your left navigation panel in the Alexa app.
6. Then select the term Groups from the menu > Create Groups.
7. Then you should enter your anticipated group name. You usually use the room names to give your group a recognizable name. If you need to group every smart item connected in the bedroom you should name your group mastered.
8. Once you have named the group you can select the devices in which you would like to add to this group. You should select Add once you have completed.

Once you have created your group in the Alexa app you can use commands via Alexa with it. If you need to use some skill you should say to Alexa "Open [skill name]" before she recognizes your request and complete it. Here is the list of sample commands you can use with your smart home devices:

"Set [Group Name] to [#]%"
"Turn on [Smart Device Name or group]"

You can manage your device scene through the desired device's companion application. You can see the scene names in the Smart Home section of the Alexa app. You can also edit Smart Groups within the Alexa Application. You can do it easily by under Groups by selecting the group you would like to edit. If you want to make changes to the name you should select the desired group and edit the text information. In case if you need to change the items within the group you should select or deselect the checkbox next to the application. And if you need to delete the grouping you should select Delete.

How to Use Your Echo Dot with Wikipedia

Wikipedia is one of the most reliable and popular resources that widespread all over the world. It gets over 500 million monthly views every day and its information is edited and updated by the users all the time.

If you like to know something new from Wikipedia the Amazon Echo Dot can also work with it without using any skill.

It is simple to use the Echo Dot in conjunction with Wikipedia. And if you want your Echo Dot to read a passage from Wikipedia you should say: "Alexa – Wikipedia [topic]". This command is meant to search the topic.

The Echo Dot will read a passage to the requested topic. But Alexa will not read the whole article, only a short passage. If you want Alexa to continue reading this article, you say "More" or "hear more".

You can also get information another way from Alexa and Wikipedia by saying: "Alexa, Wikipedia [Name of the Article]". And Alexa will read the article you need.

How to Use Your Echo Dot for Radio Programs

As you know the Amazon Echo Dot works with different media applications and you can also utilize the Dot for listening to local radio stations.

You can listen to live radio streams through the Echo Dot without any account sign up or setup, using the integration with TuneIn. If you like listening to the radio then you should create a free TuneIn Account. Having your new account, you can follow your favorite stations. They will be available when your Echo Dot is performing a search and moves them to the top of the results.

The Echo Dot is able to recognize and to find live radio stations even if the podcasts are limited to the items featured on TuneIn. If you want to begin listening to a radio station using Alexa, you should say, "Alexa, play [number on the dial] [station name]".

Besides, the Echo Dot may be used as an internet radio. Using a simple command, you can enable the radio to play within seconds. TuneIn is a defaults database for streaming radio. If you ask Alexa to play some station it will repeat the station you asked for to make sure you it is correct. Alexa may also ask for confirmation.

You should know that your Echo Dot does not come with a tuner and all radio programs are streamed via your Wi-Fi connection. The weak signal may hinder your ability to clearly listen to programs. But if your connection speeds are good, you can have good signal. You can use your Echo Dot as a bedside radio and attach headphones at leisure.

How to Use TuneIn

If you want to start listening to the radio or podcasts via your Amazon echo Dot you do not need a TuneIn account as your Echo Dot is able to do it without it. The TuneIn Library is large enough to meet any expectations and tastes. It is ready for your exploration. You should know the name of the podcast you would like to listen to and the Echo Dot is ready to play it. Here are some sample commands that you can tell to get the most out of TuneIn, using your Echo Dot:

"Alexa, play [Podcast Name] podcast on TuneIn."

"Alexa, play the podcast [insert podcast name here]."

These commands work great if you know the name of the show you are searching for.

There are also two ways you can use to search for podcasts via TuneIn. You can do it within the Alexa application or via the TuneIn Website. When you have found something you are interested in, you should use the commands above to start listening on your Echo Dot or its connected Bluetooth Speaker.

Listening to a particular podcast is easier than listening to the podcasts in a specific order. You can use the Alexa App as a remote to control which podcast should play first, second, etc. After listening to the backlog of podcasts you may be offered a show. Then you can return to using Alexa to play the newest episodes.

How to Use IHeartRadio

You can choose lots of music that you would like to listen to, access a variety of live radio stations and create your very own radio station, using this application.

IHeartRadio is able to play your favorite jams without stopping. Once you have given your station options it will find similar music to play on your station. This list of available songs includes over 20 million tracks.

It is easy to create an IHeartRadio account. You can also use your Facebook or Gmail accounts for quick creation. Once you have completed with your account you should simply link within the Alexa App to utilize with your Amazon Echo Dot.

Here are the sample commands:

"Alexa, play Fox Sports Radio on iHeartRadio."

"Alexa, open IHeartRadio"

How to Use Pandora Radio

Pandora is another radio streaming service which is able to serve as the Echo Dot's default music source unlike Spotify.

When you give the command to Alexa she must specify which streaming service to choose to play your request from. And if the service is left out she will use the default option.

If you have not updated the default Alexa will try to play the item from Amazon Music. You should navigate to the Music section of the Alexa mobile application to update your default application. You should open your settings and select 'Music & Media'. Then you should choose the button which reads "Choose Default Music Services" within this section. If you have not subscribed to Amazon Prime you need to do it to ensure your music is coming from the right application.

You should follow these to set up Pandora or your Amazon echo Dot:

1. First you should navigate to the Alexa app.
2. Then select the Menu button. You can see the button in the left corner of the application. Then select Music & Books and select Pandora.

3. Then, from the registration page, you should select the "Link your account now" Button
    1. If you have not created your account you should select "Create a Pandora Account". Then fill out the needed information to complete the registration process.
    2. If you have an account simply you should select "I have a Pandora Account". Then you should enter in your associated Pandora email address and password. Then proceed by tapping "Look Up Account".

Once you have completed this process, you will see that your current station list will appear within the Alexa Application.

If you want to utilize Pandora with the Amazon Echo Dot, you should use some commands below:

"Alexa, I like this song"

"Alexa, thumbs down this song"

"Alexa, play [Artist Name] radio on Pandora"

You should also know that usual items like Stop, Pause, resume work the same like with normal music play on Alexa.

Chapter 5: Playing Games with Your Echo Dot

The Amazon Echo Dot can be used not only for asking information you can also use it to play games. There are lots of games that you can play with your Echo Dot. Using the Alexa skills portion of the application, you can enable these games. Once you have enabled the game you would need just to say the keywords to start.

Here is the list of games:

Truth or Dare: You can play a classic game of Truth or Die with the help of Alexa. The concept of this game is when a group of people take turns asking each other "Truth or Dare?" To enable this game, just say:

"Alexa, open truth or dare"

"Alexa play truth or dare"

Bingo: You can also play Bingo but you will need bingo cards that you can download from lovemyecho.com in PDF format.

When your Echo Dot call out the bingo numbers for the entire game you should simply respond with "Next" to keep the game continue.

When you want to start playing this game you should say "Alexa, open Bingo". When you want to continue the game, just say "call the next number".

Tic Tac Toe: You can play Tic Tac Toe on your Echo Dot. It is very easy as you can remember your positioning. You should to sketch the moves while you are playing. You can recorder the moves using the following positioning:

Top Left | Top | Top Right
Left | Center | Right
Bottom Left | Bottom | Bottom Right

When you are ready to start a game with Alexa, just say "Alexa, let's play tic tac toe"

Blackjack: You can play numerous rounds of blackjack while Alexa keeps track of your bankroll. There are different versions of blackjack. For example, blackjack by Garrett Vargas starts with 5000 credits and adds and subtracts during the game.

If you don't know the rules Alexa can read them and give the basic game strategy. You can enable the game of blackjack by saying such command:

"Alexa, start a game of black jack"

Jeopardy: You can freely enable this skill as it is easy to add it from the skills section within the Alexa application to the Echo Dot. You can start game by saying, "Alexa, start Jeopardy".

This game includes lots of questions from different categories. The categories may be sports, history, travel and even pop culture. And the answers should be in the question form.

Chapter 6: Getting General Information with Your Echo Dot

If you want to know some general information you even don't need to setup any of the skills. Alexa can perform a lot of general commands. Here are the basic commands:

"Alexa, stop.": If you want Alexa to stop activity it is performing or to close out music that is playing you should say this command. It concerns such activities as playing music, playing some game or generally performing some skill.

"Alexa, turn volume to 10"/ "Alexa, volume seven.": This command enables to turn the volume up or down between zero and ten without touching the volume button. You can also say such commands like "Alexa, turn it up" or "Alexa turn it down" to control the sound.

"Alexa, please mute."/ "Alexa, please unmute.": If you need to mute and unmute the volume on the device, simple say this command.

"Alexa, cancel.": You can cancel any activity that Alexa is going to perform with this command. You can also say "stop" instead of "cancel".

"Alexa, what's my Flash Brief?": You can get news according to the settings you have made with your flash briefings in the Alexa mobile application.

"Alexa, what's headlining in the news?": You can get information about what is currently headlining in the news.

"Alexa, what's the weather for today?": You can ask about weather forecast for today or tomorrow or ask the probability of rain today by saying: "Alexa, what is the chance that it will rain today?" or "Alexa, do I need an umbrella this week?"

If you need a weather forecast for upcoming weekend you can ask: "Alexa, what's the weather for this upcoming weekend?"

While cooking or when you need it, you can ask Alexa basic measurement questions even without setting any skills. Here are the measurement questions you can ask:

"How many tea spoons in one soup-spoon?"

"Alexa, how many cups in a pint?"

"How many miles are from New York to Chicago?"

Alexa has got vast knowledge in many spheres. You can ask any kind of questions and get to know the scores of latest matches in basketball, baseball and other sport related question.

Without involving any skills, Alexa is ready to answer all your questions and she can also do minor conversions and simple math.

Easter Eggs

You should know that not all features within the Echo Dot or within Alexa are spelled out in nice detailed lists. There are things which are still left to be discovered. Easter eggs are weird phrases and jokes that Alexa will respond to. The new Easter eggs are added every day.

Here is the list of Easter Eggs that you can use with Alexa. These phrases are taken from Reddit and compiled by users of the site.

1. "Alexa, do you know Glados?"

2. "Alexa, what is the meaning of life?"

3. "Alexa, who lives in a pineapple under the sea?"

4. "Alexa, is there a Santa?"

5. "Alexa, do aliens exist?"

6. "Alexa, where do you live?"

7. "Alexa, what is love?"

8. "Alexa, what is your quest?"

9. "Alexa, do you know Hal?"

10. "Alexa, what is your favorite color?"

11. "Alexa, which comes first: the chicken or the egg?"

12. "Alexa, can you give me some money?"

13. "Alexa, do you want to fight?"

14. "Alexa, do you know the muffin man?"

15. "Alexa, where are you from?"

16. "Alexa, how much do you weigh?"

17. "Alexa, why did the chicken cross the road?"

18. "Alexa, where are my keys?"

19. "Alexa, who let the dogs out?"

20. "Alexa, how tall are you?"

21. "Alexa, why do birds suddenly appear?"

22.. "Alexa, will you be my girlfriend?"

23. "Alexa, who's the boss?"

24. "Alexa, is there life on Mars?"

25. "Alexa, do you want to go on a date?"

26. "Alexa, what are you wearing?"

27. "Alexa, give me a hug."

28. "Alexa, what is the sound of one hand clapping?"

29. "Alexa, what are you made of?"

30. "Alexa, what should I wear today?"

You can find more Easter Eggs on Amazon website or other websites.

Asking about Weather & Other General Information

Whenever you have a busy morning when you are in a hurry for work and you don't have enough time to check some things, Alexa is ready to help you with it. She can provide you with the latest information about weather so you could know what to wear and to remind you to check your phone or tell you the time. You don't need to touch your phone as Alexa can tell you all this information.

You can use the following command to get to know all necessary general information:

- *"Alexa, what's the weather in New York?" or "Alexa what's the weather?"* Alexa is able to provide you with the weather information for your current address area if you haven't a specified the city. If you have specified the city, she can give the forecast for that area.

- *Alexa, what's the time?* Alexa can tell you the current time without any extra details.
- *Alexa, what is my commute?* You can use this command if you have set your home and work address within the Alexa application. If you ask this Alexa is able to provide you with the current traffic and route information along with an estimated time.

Chapter 7: How to Use your Echo Dot with Multiple Devices

It is recommended to use the Echo Dot in conjunction with other devices. It is easy to add a new Echo Dot to the home. You can do it the same way as the initial set up of your first device.

When it's time to set up the second device you should log into the Alexa application and navigate to your settings and follow general setup instructions. It is not necessary to go through the set up process again with your second device as the new device will take on the skills of your connected device.

It is also important to place your multiple devices right to get the perfect balance in your home. It may lead to confusion if you place one device in the middle of two standing devices.

Controlling all Alexa enabled devices is easy with your voice or through the Alexa app. They are able to respond even if they have the same wake word due to ESP (Echo Spatial Perception). Some versions of the Alexa products do not require a wake word. They are Amazon Tap, Fire tablets, and Fire TV devices.

When interacting with your Echo Dot you can use the Alexa Voice Remote that it sold separately. There is also an option to change your wake word for different devices.

But you should know that not all applications are able to work in sync. All the Alexa enabled devices cannot play music at the same time for full affect. If you have Spotify as your default music source then your devices cannot play the same songs.

You also cannot sync timers and alarms between multiple devices. You should know that every Echo Dot performs independently of one another even the skills are the same between the devices. Bluetooth connections are also set separately.

Not all the function may be synced between Alexa products. But within the Alexa mobile application all the information listed under the Account section is the same for all linked devices. This information includes such options:

- Music & Media Information – It includes information from Amazon Music, Spotify, Pandora, iHeartRadio and TuneIn.
- Flash Briefings – You can get the information for where to get flash briefings from and what areas are turned on.

- Sports Update – You can get information about the teams you would like to know about.
- Traffic – It includes the home information set by the user to provide the route traffic information.
- Shopping and To-do lists
- Calendar

Chapter 8: How to Use Your Echo Dot for Various Skills

The Echo Dot can utilize a great number of Amazon Skills to prove it is truly smart home device. These skills include different categories:

- Food & Drink
- Games & Trivia
- Health & Fitness
- Lifestyle
- Local
- Movies & TV
- Music & Audio
- News
- Humor
- Productivity
- Shopping
- Smart Home
- Social
- Sports
- Travel & Transportation
- Utilities
- Weather

- Business & Finance
- Communication
- Education & Reference

Food & Drink

The Amazon Echo Dot has many skills to use for food and drink. They include items that provide current drink specials, recipes or even the means to order food. The ordering of pizza and even wings is still one of the most popular features in the food section.

Wingstop:

If you enable the Wingstop skill you will be able to order wings a cinch. You can order wings from recent orders or from your set favorites.

But first you must have a linked Wingstop account to use this skill. Using this account, you can manage your favorite orders as well as any payment information needed to make orders.

Alexa is able to guide you through the entire order process. Once you have placed your order Alexa will also provide information when your order will be available and send a confirmation email. You can enable this skill by simply saying the following commands:

"Alexa, ask Wingstop to order 4-piece spicy wing combo"
"Alexa, ask Wingstop to order my favorite"

Pizza Hut:

Using the Pizza Hut skill, you can have a pizza at your door within the hour without picking up a phone. First, you must have a linked Pizza Hut account to be able to use this skill. You can manage your favorite orders as well as any payment information needed to make orders with the help of your account. You can also order from the menu.

Before ordering from Pizza Hut you should make sure that you have a delivery address and a default payment method on your pizza hut account.

Here are simple commands to order pizza:

"Alexa, open Pizza Hut"

"Alexa, ask Pizza Hut to reorder my last order"

Domino's Pizza:

This is one of the most advertised and popular Alexa skills. You can not only place the most recent order but also to check the status of your order using the Domino's Tracker that is currently available only in the United States.

You also need an account with Dominoes to continue with order placement, like with previous skills. You should link this account in the Alexa application as well. If you want to place an order through Alexa you must have a recent order or have an Easy Order saved. You should enter all of your pertinent information like your address, credit card and phone number into your pizza profile on the Domino's website.

You will need your phone number to track your order and receive the status. It is easy to enable this application for ordering by simply saying:

"Alexa, open Domino's"
"Alexa, open Domino's and place my most recent order"

Business & Finance

Any user can find something helpful among business and finance skills of the Echo Dot, depending on his lifestyle and needs. The Echo Dot is able to perform such skill when the user can get the updated economical and insurance information. Here are some sample applications:

Capital One: You can ask about your credit card, bank account, home or auto loans using the Capital One. Using this skill, you can also easily know where you are spending the most money. The Capital One includes many commands. But you must first log into Capital One from within the Alexa application to create the linkage if you want to start using this skill.

When you want to ask about your Credit Card you should use the following Alexa commands:
"Alexa, how much did I spend at [insert store name] last week?"
"Alexa, how much did I spend last month at [insert store name]?"
"Alexa, ask Capital One what is my credit card balance."
"Alexa, ask Capital One when is my credit card bill due?"

When you want to ask about your banking account, use the following Alexa commands:
"Alexa, ask Capital One, what are my recent transactions?"
 "Alexa, ask Capital One, what is my checking account balance?"

When you want to ask about your automotive loan, use the following Alexa commands:
 "Alexa ask Capital One, what is my payoff quote?"
 "Alexa ask Capital One, when is my car loan due?"
 "Alexa ask Capital One, what is my s my car loan principal?"

When you want to ask about your home loan, use the following Alexa commands:

"Alexa, ask Capital One, when is my next mortgage payment due?"
"Alexa, ask Capital One, what is the principal on my mortgage?"

Nationwide Insurance: If you want to know the information about auto insurance products and contact information for quotes the Nationwide Alexa skill will help you with it. Here are some common statements to enable Nationwide:
"Alexa, open Nationwide"
"Tell me about primary coverages"

Real Estate

If you need to find home, to buy or rent within a specific area this application will provide you this information. To enable this application you should first create an account and sign up with Voiceter Pro. Once you have created the account and linked with Alexa you can search for homes but receive contact information from local realtors. Here are some common statements to enable Real Estate:
"Alexa, open Real Estate"
"Alexa, tell Real Estate to buy some house in Los Angeles"

Communication

Using the communication section of the skills houses items you can send messages, receive notifications and provide facts.
Here are the items that some of these skills include: A T&T messages, Programming facts, Hindi tutor and secret keeper.

AT&T Send Message:
You can use this application with a Post Paid AT&T mobile phone. But first you must connect your AT&T wireless account to provide proper work for this skill. You can add 10

frequent contacts as message recipients. Here are some
common statements to enable AT&T Send Message:
"Alexa, open AT&T"
"Alexa, ask AT&T to text my mother"
"Alexa, ask AT&T to text my son"

Message Wall:

This application enables the users of Echo products to send
anonymous message to one and another. This skill may not
be appropriate for children and they should be monitored
closely by parents if the children try to utilize it. Here are
some common statements to enable Message Wall:

"Alexa, open Message Wall"
"Alexa, what was the last message on Message Wall"

Education & Reference

This section of the Alexa skills section provides learning and
fact type skills. These skills are: quotes, word spells,

presidents and various other types. Here are some sample applications:

Computer Geek:

You can know various interesting computer facts with this skill. This application is meant to provide interesting and useful information to the user. You can enable this application free and utilize it easily. Here are some common commands to enable this application include:
"Alexa, ask Computer Geek to tell me something"
"Alexa, ask Computer Geek to give me a fact"

Read the Old Testament This Year:

Using this application, you can read the King James Version of the bible on a regular basis. This skill is designed to start on January 1 and continue throughout the year, reading a scheduled passage each day. Here are some common ways to enable this application:

"Alexa, read the Old Testament"
"Alexa, ask the Old Testament for today's reading"

"Alexa, ask Old Testament to read for November 15"

This Day in History:

This application is brought to Alexa by A&E Television Network. Using this skill, you can know random facts on things that have happen on your current date in history. You can launch this skill by saying the following commands:
"Alexa, launch This Day in History"
"Tell me about another event from August 10"

Travel & Transportation

Uber: The application Uber is designed to make it easy for a user to call for a ride any time. In order to be able to use Uber you must enable it through Alexa in a very specific way.

First, you must create or sign into your existing Uber Account before using Uber via Alexa. Once you have completed it you can use Alexa to change your default pickup location, ask for ride status or cancel an already requested ride. You can also request rides from different Uber accounts.

To enable Uber on your device you should say things like:
"Alexa, ask Uber to change my default pickup location"
"Alexa, ask Uber to request a ride"
"Alexa, ask Uber to call me an Uber SUV from work"

Music

You will also have access the Amazon music library associated with your Amazon account. If you have subscribed to Amazon Prime music, you will be available to use it as well.

You can use the free option TuneIn radio with your Echo Dot. You can connect it with Spotify after subscription. Besides, you can update your default music subscription to be Spotify within the Alexa application.

Chapter 9: Resetting the Echo Dot and Troubleshooting Issues

The Amazon Echo Dot is quite unique device but, as any kind of technology, sometimes it needs resetting. If Alexa does not respond properly to your commands or your Wi-Fi is not connecting properly you should reset your Echo Dot. Whatever streaming issues you may have with your Echo Dot your first essential step must be restarting your device. You should just press and hold down the Microphone and Volume down buttons at the same time to make restart of your Echo Dot.

You should do it until the light ring on your Echo Dot turns orange. Once it's complete the light ring should turn blue. Then it illuminates blue it will turn on and off again. Your device should be ready for regular use and you should setup Wi-Fi if needed.

Another case is when the companion application may become unresponsive.
It may happen when the skills backing up the Alexa software as your mobile application is constantly being updated. If you have received a message stating that the "The Alexa app

is offline", there are many solutions to fix this error. Here are the solutions you should follow:

1. **Restarting your mobile device** – It is a common way to fix small issues in application. You can fix any unresponsiveness using this way.
2. **Force close the application** – If you force closing the application it may also aid in solving in immediate issues. You can also have the option to clear data for the Alexa companion application in some devices if desired. As Amazon recommends you should clear the data and select "Force Stop".
3. **Uninstall and reinstall the Application** – One of the ways to clear up any issues within the Alexa application is uninstalling the application. After uninstalling the application you should navigate to your respective app store and re-download the application

How to Solve Connection & Streaming Issues with the Echo Dot

Normally your Wi-Fi connection determines the connection issues with the Echo Dot. You may have troubleshoot and rectify these issues in many ways. Here are some common fixes:

- **Restart Your Amazon Echo Dot** can be the most common fix for any connectivity issues.
- **Reduce Wi-Fi Congestion** – You can reduce your Wi-Fi congestion by turning off devices that are not being used. It will free up some much needed bandwidth on your network.
  If you raise the device from the ground or keep it away from any walls it may help in keeping the lines of connection open. If it does not solve the issue you should move your device closer to the router/modem so it may improve the connection.

- **Restart Your Network Device** – If you have some with the network connectivity of your Echo Dot you should reset the modem. It may be another way to fix when troubleshooting.

- **Contact Your Internet Service Provider** – If none of the above fixes does not help you, you should contact your Internet Service Providers. Also, if you know that it is not an issue with your Amazon Echo Dot device and you still have this problem, you should contact your Internet Service Provider for more help troubleshooting your network connection.

Bluetooth Connection Issues with Your Amazon Echo Dot

One of the complications that may arise while interacting with your Echo Dot is a Bluetooth issue. There are many things you can do to fix a Bluetooth connectivity issues and here is the list of fixes:

- **Interference** – It includes a number of various items. These are electronic devices that may block your signal. Baby monitors, microwaves and various other wireless devices may be common interference items too.

If your Bluetooth connectivity does not function properly you should move your device away from anything that may interfere with the connection.

- **Battery Life of your Mobile Device** – You should know that the battery life of your mobile device may also interfere with capability to connect by Bluetooth. You should make sure that the device has a full charge if your device has a battery that is not able to be removed. You should replace or recharge the batteries if your device has removable and (or) rechargeable batteries.

- **Delete all prior Bluetooth Devices** – If you have any connectivity issues you should clear and reconnect the Bluetooth device. It may aid in rectifying any connectivity issues. To clear your Bluetooth device, you should navigate to

  Settings within the Mobile Alexa companion application, from within the left navigation panel. Then, inside of Settings, you should select the Alexa Device that you are having issues with and select **Bluetooth** > clear.

- **Add a New Bluetooth Device** – One of the simplest ways to test if a Bluetooth connection is working properly is to delete all old devices and reconnect a new one. You can do it by selecting your Alexa device, selecting Bluetooth> Pair a New Device. When your device enters pairing mode you should select the device from your cellular device. And then Alexa will confirm if your device has been connected successfully.

Chapter 10: How Can You Use the Echo Dot

The Amazon Echo Dot is able to perform lots of things. It can helpful in any specific area of the home.

Using Your Echo Dot in the Kitchen

The Echo Dot can be helpful not only in the bedroom, living room, bathroom but also in the kitchen. It is able to perform lots of tasks to help you with working in the kitchen.

1. Maintaining your grocery list

Making any list may become easy with Alexa. You can make any kind of lists and shopping lists are the ones that are the most compatible with the Dot. You should tell Alexa the item and the list which you would like to add the corresponding item and it will be done at once. For example, you can say "Alexa, please add flour to my Grocery List"

> You can edit and update all your lists without speaking directly to Alexa within the Alexa app. You should just select Shopping & To Do lists.

2. How to Use Alexa to Convert Kitchen Units

One of the most helpful skills while cooking is that Alexa is able to convert units to match an altered serving size of a recipe. Sometimes it is hard to do when your hands are busy. And Alexa can help you with it.

You should know that Alexa is able to answer general metric and simple questions. You can simply say, "Alexa convert 5 cups to pints" and she will do it for you.

3. How to Use Alexa to Make Your Morning Coffee

You can do so many things with all of the smart home integrations and even make your morning coffee. You just need to achieve a simple drip coffee maker and a smart switch. To enable this skill, you should go into IFTTT and create a recipe to run on the smart switch plug. To provide a proper work, you must add your coffee grounds and water to your coffee pot the night before. This is one thing that Echo Dot cannot do for you. Once it is done when you wake up and you should say your trigger phrase and the coffee should be ready when you are.

4. How to Use Alexa to Start Timers

Timers are very helpful in the kitchen. You can use them to determine quickly when food is done or when your cake must come out of the oven. You should simply say "Alexa, start a new time for 15 minutes from now". When 15 minutes have passed you will hear the Echo Dot's speaker until you stop it.
You can also set multiple timers at once with Alexa. It does not matter what is the length of time, you can check the status of your timers by simply asking Alexa. You can also cancel timers if it is needed.

5. Use the Echo Dot to Control appliances

IFTTT included lots of integrated appliances. You are able to control all the devices integrated with your Echo Dot. For example, you can control your dishwasher, oven or even your slow cooker with Alexa enabled device.

But first you will need to create applets within the appropriate appliance service in IFTTT to enable these devices. These applets usually use Amazon Alexa as the trigger.

6. Use Alexa to generate Recipe ideas
One of the things that can be handled through the Alexa skills is finding recipes. There are lots of skills that you can use while searching for unique recipes using your Echo Dot.
Here are some skills:

Recipe Finder by Ingredient:
You can find recipes based on the items that they currently have in their possession, using this skill. You can ask about the type of dish that you want to make and get ideas from this application. You should say some alike commands to enable this skill:
"Alexa, ask Recipe Finder by Ingredient what kind of sandwich can I make with Swiss cheese"
"Alexa, ask Recipe Finder by Ingredient what I can make with potatoes and mushrooms"

Trending Recipes & Food:

You can get the top recipes on Reddit Food within the last 24 hours with this skill. You will get the requested recipes via a link in a card in the Alexa application. You should remember that this content must be user submitted. You can say some alike commands to enable this skill:

"Alexa, can I have the fifth recipe from Trending
Recipes"
"Alexa, get the latest recipe from Trending Recipes"
"Alexa, give me the most recent recipe in Trending
Recipes" recipe

Best Recipes:

You can enable this skill free. Using this skill, you can tell
Alexa what ingredients you have to work with and it will
provide you with three ingredients that suit your needs.
You can narrow down the recipe choice by time of day or
dish type. It concerns the options of breakfast, lunch or
dinner. You can browse recipes and choose the one which
is most attractive to you. You should say some commands
like these ones to enable this skill:

"Alexa, please open Best Recipes"
"Alexa, ask best recipes what's for lunch"
"Alexa, ask best recipes what's for dinner"

These are not all the recipe skills that you can use with the Echo Dot. You can find other applications in the skills library that are able to give you interesting cooking ideas.

7. How to Use Alexa to Count & Maintain Calories

If you keep a diet or you like healthy lifestyle Alexa is able to help you with counting calories without enabling a skill. She is able to tell you how many calories certain foods have. You should remember that Alexa does not know about all foods but she knows the basics.
Alexa also knows nutritional information like carbohydrates. If it is a wide spread information she will tell you all about food. If you ask about generic foods you can get back lots of information.

8. How to Use Alexa to find wine Pairing Information

Wine Buddy is a skill to give the best pairing options with certain dishes. You should simply enable Wine Buddy in the Alexa application.

It is easy to use this skill by asking your Echo Dot "Alexa, what can I serve with fried salmon?" And it will give you recommendations what would match with your chosen dish.

This skill is getting more and more advanced so you should keep the requests basic to get the accurate answers.

9. Use Alexa for Drink recipes & Ideas

If you are planning some holiday party and you need some beverage ideas Alexa is able to help you with that. She will suggest a number of cool refreshing cocktail to match your mood and company. Here are the skills that you can use: Easy Cocktail, Suggest Me a Cocktail and Mixologist. The beverages in this category are not suitable for all ages so the users should be age 21 and up.

Easy Cocktail: This skill provides recipes for various cocktails. You can
enable this skill by saying such commands:
 "Alexa, ask easy cocktail how to make a classic margarita"
 "Alexa, ask Easy Cocktail how you make a fuzzy navel"

Using Your Echo Dot to Tell Bedtime Stories

If you have no time to tell bedtime story to your children the Echo Dot can do it for you as it is able to keep children entertained with the Short Bedtime Story skill. The duration of each of the stories within this skill is about 30 seconds to one-minute long. They may also include the name of your choice to be more personalized.

You can find several different stories in the application of different plots and story twists. There are even stories related to popular Minions. You can choose the stories that take place in a galaxy or Alexa is able to tell you a story about a kid getting elected as president. Some stories may not be suitable for bedtime but other ones are good enough to lull your child.

Information on the Latest Features

It is always easy to understand what updates have been made to Alexa. Sometimes you might need to read a newsletter or subscribe to some email listing but it is not compulsory. You should just say "Alexa, what new features do you have?"

You should also know when something is added or pushed to the Echo Dot, Alexa will explain you what it is. You should simply ask for an explanation and you will get it.

Workouts

The Workout may also become quick and easy process with your Amazon Echo Dot. You will not have any excuses why you can't do small workout in during the day after enabling the 7 Minute Workout skill. If you don't have time or you don't like gyms it is a great alternative to use 7 Minute Workout.

You can enable the "7-Minute Workout" skill within the Amazon Alexa companion mobile application and you will get a quick workout that takes 7 minutes to complete. This workout is perfect for getting energized before your working day starts or you can get in some quick activity before bed.

Once you have enabled it in the Alexa app, you can start your workout by saying "Alexa, start 7-minute workout". These workouts include so many kinds of exercises like jumping jacks, pushups, wall sits, squats, and much more.

You can also see the images inside the Alexa application just to make sure that you are doing all of the moves correctly.

Always Add More Skills to Learn More

Originally the Echo Dot already has a number of skills enabled. Some of the them are basic and the other skills may be enabled within the Alexa app to take your Echo Dot on another level.

You can enable thousands of skills online, from the Alexa app or even from talking directly to Alexa. You can update new skills every day.

If you want to get a complete listing of skills you should simply open the Alexa app, choose the menu button and select the word Skills. You can browse the skills by category and enable the items you like most of all.

If you want to learn more cooking and various recipes, you should simply enable the Mom's Cooking skill. Using this skill, you can get recipes for everything. You should just say: "Alexa, ask Mom's cooking for a cookie recipe".

You can control everything that the Echo Dot is able to perform. Alexa has got a great diversity of categories and activities. Anybody can find something according to his taste and interest. It is also important to remember the commands or the names of the applications associated with them to enable certain skills.

Ask My Buddy

Ask My Buddy is a useful emergency alert system that you can use when you need some help. This application may be configured to call a friend, family member or caretaker. You can also send a text message, email or make an actual phone call with this application.

This application proves that Alexa can be also a concerned assistant. Especially this skill is good for children, individuals who are sick or senior citizens. This skill is connected directly to the functionality of the mobile device.

This skill shows that Alexa is able to become more than virtual assistant device. The software has been incorporated

into wheelchairs and it might be soon an abundance of other medical devices.
The Ask My Buddy skill was included in Alexa Customers Top Pick list for 2016.

Fitbit

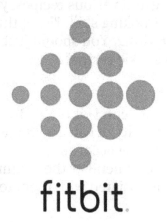

Fitbit was one of the most downloaded applications last Christmas in 2015. This skill provides information about your activity, sleep patterns and various other information related to your health. And it also provides measurements like your resting heart rate.

You should know that the Integration with Alexa and the Echo Dot cannot sync or even log water and food consumption for this moment. It will be changed in the near future to make logging food and drink easier.

Find Your Phone

If you have lost your cellular device and there is nobody around to call you. Don't worry. Alexa is able to help you with it too.

Alexa has got many various options to accomplish this. There are some skills that require the installation of a companion application on the cellular device and some others have the ability to ring the device on command. Once you have enabled the skill by configuring the setting with the Alexa applicant, you should simply say "Alexa, find my phone" and your device will ring loudly even if it was on silent.

IFTTT recipes may be also helpful if you set them. But you should make sure that triggers are in place if you lose your device and the key phrase must be spoken.

Conclusion

The Amazon Echo Dot is able to perform a great variety of skills and tasks. It can stream music and Podcasts from different sources including Amazon Prime, Spotify, IHEartRadio, TuneIn or Pandora.

The Amazon Echo Dot is Amazon's newest Alexa enabled powerhouse. It can be awakened by speaking one of the wake words like Alexa, Amazon or Echo. You can turn off the Echo Dot by tapping the tapping the designated microphone button atop the devices.

This smart gadget is able to look up facts, tell jokes and give general information. You can set alarms and timers for your activities, make to-do lists, read books, control your home and many other things.

Beside all this features, the Echo Dot may be used as a hub for all your smart home tasks. The list of appliances that work with the Echo Dot is growing. Here are some of the most common utilities:

- Nexia smart home
- Crestron smart home
- Lutron Lighting sets
- Haiku smart lights

- Belkin Switches
- SmartThings home platform
- Wink home platform
- Insteon home platform
- August Lock
- Scout Security system
- Ecobee3 Thermostat
- Philips Hue Bulb
- LIFX Bulbs
- Ledvance Bulbs
- Nest Thermostat
- Logitech Harmony Hub entertainment controller
- Control4 smart home

The new items that will work with the Amazon Echo Dot and Alexa are being added every day. There are over 3000 skills which enable Alexa to do lots of tasks.

The Echo Dot is able to do something more than the Tap and the Echo. For example, it can connect external speakers and audio systems via Bluetooth or cable line-in connection.

The Amazon Echo Dot is also able to recognize your voice and it can also give you the option of adding various audio features.

Even if the Echo Dot doesn't come with a line cable it can perform a lot of options and it is really worth the money. The Amazon Echo Dot has the same qualities as the full sized Echo just in a smaller size. And when loud music playing, it is able to pick up your voice and respond your questions and requests.

The Echo Dot also makes it easier to get music. You can play selected songs and albums on the external speakers. And unlike the Echo Dot itself these devices are not "always on". But you can give verbal commands to Alexa in order to re-enable Bluetooth speakers.

Despite the new competition emerging everyday Amazon's devices such as the Amazon Echo, Amazon Tap and the Amazon Echo Dot stay in the lead for smart home/virtual assistant devices.

Among big variety of alternatives to suite of Alexa-based products none is able to match the functionality and compatibility of the Amazon Alexa products. And the Amazon Echo Dot is a small device that can do big things.

Thank you for reading. I hope you enjoy it. I ask you to leave your honest feedback.

I think next books will also be interesting for you:

<u>Amazon Echo</u>

Amazon Echo Guide

Amazon Echo Guide

The Ultimate Amazon Echo User Guide for Your Smart Home with Alexa

John Edwards